Wales at Water's Edge

Wales at Water's Edge

A Coastal Journey

JEREMY MOORE & JON GOWER

Gomer

To all those in the green movement who are making the world
a better place *JM*

To my great friend, Peter Florence *JG*

Published in 2012 by Gomer Press, Llandysul, Ceredigion SA44 4JL
www.gomer.co.uk

ISBN 978 1 84851 242 9

A CIP record for this title is available from the British Library

Book and jacket design: Rebecca Ingleby Davies, mopublications.com

This book is published with the financial support of the
Welsh Books Council, and the Countryside Council for Wales

Printed and bound in Wales at Gomer Press, Llandysul, Ceredigion

Cyngor Cefn Gwlad Cymru
Countryside Council for Wales

jacket photograph: **Bardsey Island**
opposite page: **Taf/Tawe estuary**
overleaf: **Penarth**
opposite Foreword: **Llanddwyn Island**
opposite Introduction: **Penderi oak woods**

Contents

Foreword

The Welsh Government's decision to back the creation of an all-Wales Coast Path was a bold affirmation of our potential as a nation. Completing the project is a proud achievement for the local authorities, contractors, community groups, volunteers and those who co-ordinated the effort – the staff of the Countryside Council for Wales.

The quality of our landscape is our biggest economic asset, and the path will welcome visitors from across the globe. It's an iconic addition to Wales's green infra-structure, it defines the shape of Wales and gives us access to its nature. But it's our experience as users of the path that matters – and everyone who walks the path will see and feel something different. Photographs will be taken, memories will be recorded in notebooks.

But *Wales at Water's Edge* transcends. It is a work of art, an astonishing synergy of words and images. The two artists understand Wales – Jeremy Moore through the lens as Wales's foremost landscape photographer, Jon Gower through his words as Wales's most literate environmentalist. Jeremy captures perspectives, elements and scales that elude most other photographers. Jon effortlessly weaves history, literature and wildlife observation into a matching soundscape.

Their interpretation of Wales's coastline will inspire us all to experience the beauty of Wales for ourselves. We will socialise, learn and revitalise along its 870 miles. And after our exertions, we will return to its pages, to see – maybe – something we missed, but which Jeremy and Jon saw when they were at the Water's Edge.

Morgan Parry, Chair, Countryside Council for Wales

Introduction

This is a journey around the Welsh coast, going clockwise from the south-eastern corner, starting under a very modern road crossing on the banks of the Severn estuary and ending with another muddy gape of river mouth and a bridge-border with England. Here the meandering Dee washes rather more industrial shores in the north east, a place of power stations and factories overlooking super-rich bird feeding grounds.

Between these two estuaries is a coast about as varied and various as it gets – crinkled, crimped, crenellated and corrugated – holidaymakered and lighthoused, dolphin-blessed, wind-sculpted and always wave-surrounded. In fact it's a wave-and-wind *generated* coast where aeons of storm and buffet, ebb and flow, have created its variegated tapestry, its combs of jutting rock, its secret caves and soft sands, all testament to an endless, timeless struggle – between the land for permanence, and the sea for dominance.

This wondrous coast is a place to walk, prog or beachcomb, to meditate, observe wild birds on the wing or savour profusions of flowers in their season, or just simply be. This peninsular peregrination of ours takes in cove and cave, headland and pleasure park, industrial zone and wildlife refuge. Drenched in marine light, open to all weathers, sculpted by time and gentle moon-drawn tide, the Welsh coast is both land edge and sea access, the end of things and the beginning.

Jeremy Moore has photographed the coast in all seasons. I have walked it from summer through autumn and into winter. We have seen different things and been so often delighted by both the commonplace and unexpected. We'd like to share them with you.

Jon Gower

1 Severn to Neath
From the World and its Madness

Near Barry

The mighty river Severn has *disappeared*, as if someone has somehow created an instant dam upstream, somewhere near its source on Pumlumon and stoppered its flow. In truth the reason is a trifle more pedestrian: it's high summer and rainfall is sparse. Here, near the mouth of the river, it's a state of such low tide that seawater is a very distant prospect indeed. What freshwater there is flows down slowly to meet the brine through creeks and runnels: the expanse of exposed sand and mud glistens like an enormous polytunnel.

We are *under* the second Severn Crossing, an elegant strung-steel symbol of the modern age, its cables resembling a sailing ship, or an enormous Aeolian harp, plucking high-pitched melody out of the wind.

Overhead the huge wires thrum with traffic flow, but down here a group of enthusiasts is keeping tradition alive: these are the last traditional salmon fishermen of the Severn. They sweep their home-made, horseshoe-shaped lave nets through the water, to surprise a salmon. It's a technique practised here as far back as the 1630s.

Before he heads out to the fishing grounds at Black Rock, Llanwern steelworker Martin Morgan dons thigh-high waders. Optimistic, he picks up a yew knocker for dispatching the fish and a snouter, a lanyard to hang a salmon round his shoulders. Not that he's had much use for it recently. This season it looks as if all the fishermen might net seven fish. In total.

Martin, an affable man with a palpable enthusiasm for the estuary, inherited his skills from his great-great-grandfather William Corbin, and was taught by his uncles on his mother's side. They showed him how to create the reams of the net from willow fronds and fashion a rock staff from a pole of ash, which prods the sand in front of him much as a blind person uses a stick.

The last traditional salmon fishermen of the Severn

Not that Martin works entirely blind in his watery world. The netters have their own maps of the estuary, marking Lady Bench Reef, the Black Bedouins Reef, the marl-coloured Lighthouse Veer or the shipping channel known as 'The Shoots'. But he also works the waters by instinct, decoding the water's surface. He can look for the 'knife' of a salmon's dorsal fin slicing through, or the 'loom' or wake of a salmon swimming away from him. Martin maintains that the estuary is an open book if you only know how to read it, but few have the necessary patience, or, let's face it, the bravery to plosh out in thigh-high water to learn how to read.

I tell Martin about some coracle men I once met on the Tywi where it becomes tidal near Carmarthen. One of them told me about his colleague's ability to dandle a hand in the river and 'listen' to the river, and to do so so attentively that he was able to hear when the tide was turning near its mouth at Llansteffan or be able to listen to the song of a sewin, or sea trout, running upstream. Here was a man entirely in tune with his environment. Then, one day he woke up unable to use his innate gift, or, as his friend sadly put it 'he'd gone deaf in his right hand.'

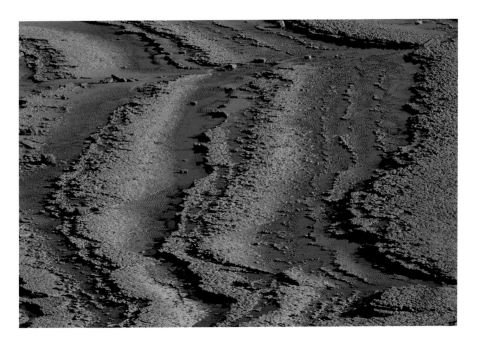

Martin has pulled on his waders by now and has to leave me behind. It's dangerous work. Running at five or six knots the water can easily take your feet from under you. There are other dangers, too, such as Black Fog, the subject of old fishermen's warnings. One day, Martin's brother Richard was out in the channel when a mysterious mist came out of nowhere. Richard had the wherewithal to take a compass reading and prod his way steadily all the way back to shore. Lived to tell his tale.

It's a schoolboy saw that the Severn has the second highest tidal range in the world after the Bay of Fundy in Newfoundland, which means that high tides can be very high and low tides very low and there's a huge gap of fifteen metres, or fifty feet, in between.

It's the Severn river that has shaped the Gwent Levels, those south Walian fenlands, east of Cardiff and either side of Newport. Reclaiming and draining has been a feature of the area since the time of the Roman legions. Although the area is crossed by natural drainage – principally the River Usk with its broad tidal estuary, the rivers Rhymney and Ebbw, and the Goldcliff Pill – the greater part of the levels has been the subject of artificial drainage schemes, creating, in effect polders such as those of the Netherlands. The flat and fertile farmlands of the Caldicot Level and the Wentloog Level are thus locked in behind sturdy sea walls. But despite the knowledge of hydrologists and the tenacity of dyke erectors, nature can still exert an awesome supremacy. The church of Saint Mary Magdalene in Goldcliff contains a brass plaque, commemorating the Great Flood of 1607 when a tsunami-style tidal wave drowned 2000 people along the shores of the Bristol Channel.

Despite the encroaching conurbations of Cardiff and Newport, the Levels retain more than a modicum of magic. This remains a strange, watery and waterlogged landscape – a place of skulking moorhens and graceful lapwings – drained by channels known

Limestone coastline, near Southerndown

as reens which are fed by small depressions in field surfaces known as grips. There is, indeed, an entire marshy lexicon for the Levels: there are gouts where reens meet and coffer gouts where they cross; pills where the major reens discharge either into tidal channels or the estuary itself, while the water levels of the reens are controlled by sluices or stanks.

These reens are miniworlds of wildlife, of water ferns and straight ranks of pollarded willows, with spooked heads of leaves and droops of filmy branches draping down toward the ditches. These irridesce with dragonflies which settle on water crowfoot, or on stands of frogbit and growth of fool's watercress. In early summer, hawthorn throws down the white confetti of its petals, while later in the year its berries provide fine outdoor dining for winter thrushes such as redwings and fieldfares.

One of the most curious and haunting pieces of Welsh archaeological evidence are some late Mesolithic human footprints found at Goldcliff, where they were preserved in estuarine clay. They trace men, women and children walking into the estuary, footprints literally left in the sands of time.

The lagoons at nearby Uskmouth used to be the settling beds for fly ash from the power station but nowadays they're home for dabbling ducks such as mallard. Here, the wind soughs through the reeds, a sibilant brushing sound as it passes through the desiccated stalks and feathery seed-heads.

On a good day – and this is a very good one – you might see a short-eared owl, but today there are six of them, their long wings trailing almost languorously over the short, tough, salt marsh grasses. One of them perches on a rotten post and turns startling lemon eyes at me. These are daylight hunters, intent on voles or delicious shrews, which are devoured alfresco, the small bodies kebabed by owl talons.

As I walk past the metal East Usk lighthouse, pewter clouds part and a slow stroboscope of light illuminates Somerset and Devon on the other side of the Bristol Channel. I scan the reeds, looking for bearded tits – but all I get is a quick glimpse of a disappearing wren. It seems to make a small chuckling sound as it dives into reed litter. Maybe I need therapy.

Over on the other side of the Usk is the place to get some.

The elusive bearded tit at Uskmouth

Here stands the white, squat West Usk lighthouse, built in 1821. It's now a quirky bed and breakfast, with a flotation tank and a Mongolian yurt. Although the out-of-town shopping malls of Newport, with their permanent two-for-one deals aren't that far away, here, on the edge of the mud, you feel at one remove from the world and its madness.

The lower Usk is a muddy place, its banks looking like cut liver, gleaming as if on a butcher's slab. As it cuts past Caerleon and skirts the eastern rim of Newport, running like liquid lead past the Riverfront Theatre, the river constantly deposits silty alluvium. When they were building this theatre they discovered the remains of a medieval ship in the mud, very well preserved and one of the best examples of its kind. This cross between a caravel and a Viking longboat was trading with Portugal in the 15th century, as evidenced by the coins they found on board and the items of cargo such as stone cannon balls, large pieces of cork and Portuguese pottery. The mud which is so good at preserving ancient ships also makes the lower river reaches

treacherous to cross, which explains why it was necessary to build a transporter bridge across the Usk at the very end of the 19th century. Its main purpose was to transport workers to the new Lysaghts steelworks, while still allowing high-masted ships access to the docks.

The Newport Transporter Bridge is a highly visible landmark and arguably the finest of its kind, the towers standing 645 feet apart and rising 242 feet above road level. It has two high towers supporting a track from which a platform or gondola is suspended to carry passengers or vehicles and is electrically powered, the gondola being pulled across by a cable wound round a drum. It certainly beats trying to manoeuvre a boat between banks of glutinous mud.

As you approach Cardiff, walking the high sea wall, you'll see a part of the landscape that simply wasn't there a decade ago. The Lamby Way landfill site is now a gently undulating hill, hiding a mulch of newspapers and an unendingness of plastic. You might happen to spot a falconer with his saker falcon, a small bird of prey much prized by desert hunters in places such as the Gulf States: there they are used to hunt Houbara bustard, here they dissuade gulls. The Rhymney meets the sea between this gargantuan rubbish tip and the housing estates of Splott and Adamsdown. In this edgeland you'll also find the last two working docks in the city, bringing in concentrated orange juice where once they exported the lion's share of the world's coal.

The Cardiff Bay of today is far removed from the coal-freighter jammed docks of yesteryear when, legend has it, you could walk from one dockside to another on ships sardined next to each other. It is now all showy architectural lines, such as the Atradius credit insurance office building with its clever mix of curves, cleaving the air like a ship's prow.

With the creation of the Cardiff Bay barrage, inundating the dunlin and redshank feeding-grounds of the Taff and Ely

A saker falcon on the fist at Lamby Way

estuaries, the city severed its connection with the sea. It still strikes one as a retrograde step, when a bit of forward thinking could have created a modern European capital city with a nature reserve in the middle.

Stand on the barrage itself, looking back on the city's relatively squat skyline and you'll see that there are few skyscrapers, very little of the 'irresistible verticality' of say, Manhattan, and only a few prominent buildings jockeying for attention. There is the five-star St David's Hotel, rising on a promontory next to the Cardiff Bay Wetlands, where, in winter, snipe probe the shallows and kingfishers plunge in a halcyon flash, and, in summer, needling flocks of swifts and swallows dine, open-gaped, on the wing. Older, smaller but no less imposing is the red-bricked Harbour Master's Office, with a south facing balcony where the eponymous master could once enjoy the spectacle of boats coming and going. Behind it rises the golden armadillo hump of the Wales Millennium Centre, with its 2000-seat theatre and permanent home for Welsh National Opera, which rather overshadows Sir Richard Rogers's home for the National Assembly, Y Senedd.

You can walk to Penarth nowadays across the barrage. Or take the water bus. It takes you into a genteel world. The erection in 1885 of the 650-foot-long pier in Penarth, originally built of cast iron with a timber deck, was destined to be a blessing for the area's rod and line fishermen, that patient breed, who are happy to wait in all weathers for their catch.

Steamer traffic was always the mainstay of the pier, with craft such as the *Waverley* taking leisure traffic across the Bristol Channel to Minehead and Ilfracombe. Out in the channel, the islands of Steep Holm, in England and Flat Holm, in Wales, register the weather: sometimes they're in clear view, sometimes rain-swept out of sight. Due to their remoteness from the land you'd think these islands made good homes for hermits. St Cadoc lived on Flat Holm for seven long years while St Gildas

set up shop on Steep Holm. Every few years they would meet to swap notes, maybe exchange recipes for what to do with raw gulls' eggs.

Flat Holm has had a lighthouse since 1737, marking out a place of many marine dangers, such as the string of rocks called the Wolves. It also has a sanatorium, familiarly referred to as a cholera hospital. There are also barracks and a gun emplacement, built as defence against the French. And gulls, a mewling, squawking abundance of them, with three to four thousand nesting pairs of lesser black-backed gulls, whitewashing the place with their guano.

So, out at sea, two saintly islands. Onshore, another benediction comes in the shape of Nicola's Coffee and Juice Bar, open in all weathers. While St Andrew is the patron saint of fishermen then Nicola Morgan, with her warming drinks and ready smile,

'In these stones horizons sing'

Nicola Morgan at Penarth pier

is a little blessing in her self as she sells both cappuccinos *and* fishing bait. Little wonder the Penarth Sea Angling Club made her an honorary member. In the lee of the elegant Pavilion – now the subject of a bold regeneration scheme – some of Nicola's customers happily tell their fishy tales. The catch here is various: autumn and winter catches of whiting and cod along with a few strap conger, pouting, poor cod and flounder; summer runs of bass, silver eels and mullet.

Barry Docks have their best days behind them, yet the days of rabid entrepreneurism must have been extraordinary. A bill to create a dock at Barry, with a railway link, was passed in 1884, having been vigorously promoted by the hyper-energetic coal owner, David Davies from Llandinam. It had many advantages over its nearby rival, Cardiff's Bute Docks. Because it was connected with the open sea via a deep entrance waterway, Barry didn't have to be scoured and dredged at great cost, and it could accommodate newer and bigger ships. Two years after it opened almost four million tonnes passed out into the Severn Sea. Ten years later, in 1901 Barry had supplanted Cardiff as the world's largest coal port. As coal declined so too did the fortunes of Barry but even after the second world war it welcomed imports of bananas – and the sight of Geest ships was a familiar one – but by century's end Dock No 1 was being converted into waterside apartments. The railway sidings are now given over to the buddleia, or butterfly bush, an alien invader.

As the docks declined tourism took up some of the slack, and the 1920s saw development of leisure facilities and the swimming Lido at the Knap. A Butlins camp followed in the 1960s, although all that's left of that red-coated jollity is a rather down-at-heel amusement park at Barry Island, where seabirds nest on the rides.

The very name Atlantic College connects this international residential school with the sea. Each year about 350 young people from over 80 different nations and from a wide range of backgrounds, cultures and creeds, congregate to attend college at St Donat's. They learn sea skills as well as book learning, so wet suits and kayaks complement physics and languages.

The castle has had some other interesting inhabitants over the years. The astonishingly powerful media magnate William Randolph Hearst – whose life formed the basis for Orson Welles's classic film study of *Citizen Kane* – saw photographs of the castle in *Country Life* magazine: the property was duly bought and revitalized by Hearst in 1925 as a gift to his long-term mistress, the Hollywood actress Marion Davies. Hearst built two new grand rooms for entertaining and imported a fair tonnage of medieval structures from both England and France. He held his own *eisteddfodau* here, with cowled men standing in for druids.

Meadow pipits are being tossed into the air along the high coastal verge as I head west from the lighthouse at Nash Point, just past the intriguingly named promontory, Castell y Dryw, the wren's castle. At Nash there is a lighthouse, built in 1832 to mark the perilous sandbanks off the point at the entrance to the Bristol Channel. It might not have been built were it not for the ferocious public outcry after the *Frolic*, a passenger steamer, was wrecked off here in 1830 with considerable loss of life.

This is a bracing walk, with fine geological striations to see, made up of limestone about 335 million years old and packed in parts with ancient pieces of coral best revealed at Southerndown – evidence of the monsoonal climate in Wales way back when more tropical seas washed onshore. If it's shelter you're after – if the winds are really gusting in – then there's hardly a finer place in the country than the walled garden, all that's left of Dunraven Castle, once seat of the powerful landowning Earls of Dunraven. The beach at Dunraven, with its surf-washed pebbles is lovely in winter and there's a semi-tropical feel to the little stretch of woodland that reaches almost to the shore at Trwyn y Witch, the witch's point. You can then walk back in a loop. I'd encourage you to do so, for entirely pleasurable reasons. It's more than coincidence that this trek ends at the Plough and Harrow, a perfect hostelry, with an open fire and Otley bitter from Pontypridd.

Tusker Rock, off the coast at Ogmore has a Viking name, evidence that these ferocious Norsemen didn't just harass Anglesey and Pembrokeshire's religious communities. These sea pirates would shark in from the open water, their early location finders fixed on food as well as other booty, for they had been driven here by overpopulation and dwindling resources in their native

The mouth of the Ebbw, near Newport

Scandinavia – like thrushes driven south to feed on bloody berries. In Glamorgan the sighting of a raven was considered unlucky even in living memory, and it's perhaps no coincidence that the Viking ships sailed under the sign of the raven. In this area, folk memory, or perhaps folk fear, dwindles and dies slowly.

Westwards, ever westwards. By the time the river Ogmore reaches the sea, it's passing though a landscape of high dunes, indeed Wales's highest dunes are found at Merthyr Mawr, a final stretch of emptiness before reaching the rollercoasters, corn dogs and static caravans of Porthcawl.

Porthcawl is a place already brilliantly chronicled by another writer, Robert Minhinnick, so I won't be pausing here long. It's

his turf and he's the guvnor. In his *Fairground Attraction* he bemoans the summer days lost to the mist. 'So many autumn days have been lost to the sea-fret, the fog settling on us like arsenic's dead-white pearls, and people looming out it, suddenly mysterious, all of us together, in fog's freemasonry, the sea a rumour, the air a saline drip.' Thousands of stoic miners used to take the air, filling their lungs with salt air during the annual holiday, miners' fortnight, knowing that soon they'd be back in the dark, picking at the earth.

I like taking my two daughters to Porthcawl's Coney Island, which shares with its New York namesake the hovering fat globules in the air coming off the burger grills. You walk past the Megablitz and a chance to see your future glisten in the silvery palms of Madam Xeena. Elena and Onwy love the donkey rides, a slow, ponderous plod along the sands which in their young minds must be akin to crossing Colorado by mule train. Luckily they're too young for the Beach Party, the centrifugal ride that tosses you in the air like NASA training for speed freaks.

Soon country meets industry. The Kenfig National Nature Reserve is a marvellous place, where you can sit near Kenfig Pool and pretend to be Henry Thoreau, meditating in Massachussetts on the edge of Walden Pond. Just as Walden itself turns out to be no remote rural idyll, set as it is on the edge of the city of Concord, so too is Kenfig set among dunes where you can only pretend to be lost, for the coking ovens and high chimneys of Port Talbot steelworks are seldom far away. Oddly, where dainty butterflies such as skippers and small blues flutter by nowadays, there used to be a busy town in medieval times, now buried in the sand.

The walk to the coast from the information centre takes you past one of Wales's most historic houses, Sker House, and an oddity in being a major house in such an isolated situation. This former grange of Neath Abbey is owned by Neil Ferguson the Harvard economics professor who has been returning its

Mugshot: Elvis Presley at Porthcawl

grand hall and enormous chimneystacks to their former glory after years of phthisis and dereliction.

As you progress across rabbit-shorn grassland, you'll often see wheatears, at least in spring and summer. Their names have nothing to do with ears, but rather, in Old English, with their white arses, which flash as the birds hop from boulder to boulder, from sand hump to sand hump. The dune system here, as elsewhere, is one of Wales's most temporary habitats, built at the fearful whim of wind and tide and just as summarily wiped away. One gale can toss up huge banks of sand but another series of sustained gusts with attendant surge can just as swiftly raze them away. From Tudor times the dunes here have been on the move, so plants on the seaward side need to send down deep roots and hug their shifting ground tightly, and be resilient enough to cope with all the lime in the broken sea shells, withstand ripping, scything winds and occasionally being buried alive under sand-drift.

The sharp blades and elegant plumes of marram show it to be the toughest frontiersman. People have long recognized its value as a stabilizer of dunes: in 1561, for instance, a law was passed which stopped people from picking it at Newborough on Anglesey. Yet there are smaller, stubborner plants even than the marram, such as prickly saltwort, sea rocket and sand sedge, all seemingly immune to the effects of salt and more salt: these are the pioneer species that help create the first advance guard of tiny dunes immediately above the tide line.

Once inside the undulating world of the dunes the thrum of the M4 and the presence of nearby heavy industry dims and diminishes. I like picking berries in the dune slacks, or chancing upon an apple tree, luscious with late fruit, or sitting down under the hovering umbrella of a kestrel's wings, as it metronomes the air, spying the grass for the least jig of a shrew.

Then, for a brief while, one can feel like Henry David Thoreau, fully at one with the world as he sat at the edge of a pond in America:

Let us first be as simple and well as Nature ourselves,
dispel the clouds which hang over our brows, and take
up a little life into our pores.

A Margam sunset

The transporter bridge at Newport

Cardiff Bay Barrage at Penarth

Port Talbot

Port Talbot

2 **Neath to Amroth**

The Tang
of Laver Bread

Rhossili

Crossing the Neath by car over the high M4 road bridge – a trapeze for traffic – heading for Swansea, takes you over edgeland, a liminal world between human influence and natural shaping, a place where nature gets raggedy and prefabricated light industrial units grow like ragweed.

The Neath flows rustily underneath us and is surprisingly navigable, even by container-laden traffic, with docks at Briton Ferry. Companies such as Briton Ferry Stevedoring still import and export here. They handle vessels up to 6,500 tonnes carrying steel, precious metals, aggregates, timber and coal.

Briton Ferry became a very active centre for ship-breaking after the Second World War: the HMS *Bermuda* was dismantled at the so-called Giant's Grave, while the area had already benefited for many years from the creation of a floating dock, designed by that Victorian über engineer Isambard Kingdom Brunel, and which opened in 1861. This was made up of an inner floating dock and an outer tidal basin and extended over 73 hectares or 180 acres.

The dunes on the western side of the Neath rivermouth are bunkered and flagged. This is the Swansea Bay Golf Club course, set in Swansea Burrows where the fen orchid still blooms beautifully if you have but patience enough to seek it out among the fairways. The course hugs the shore as you approach the gargantuan Amazon warehouse, with its fleet of continent-crossing lorries parked outside, literally voluminous traffic.

As the new city skyline starts to resemble bold lines on a graph, you go past a defunct car plant where Linamar pulled out in 2010, taking the work to Mexico – and, ironically, seeing as this was once the main drag along which the city's automotive industry flourished, you'll walk past the flag-emblazoned automobile dealers with their permanent sales proclaimed by drooping plastic pennants. A very high fence bars access to the docks to all but orang utans with wire cutters. Sadly the Swansea Cork ferry, which used to berth here, adding its funnel to the maritime skyline, has recently been withdrawn from service, a victim of the chill economic winds that blow. It was a boat service that kept the city connected, international, resolutely maritime.

Then it's the Scandinavian clean lines of the SA1 redevelopment, awash with latte, with its shiny new office blocks, hotels and sleek apartment blocks. I'm not sure what to make of the advert selling Sunday lunches – 'Grab a grannie: all you can eat, £9.99.' Sounds a mite cannibalistic. I'll opt for a sandwich.

As you edge in towards the city proper, sandy paths hemmed in by stands of sea buckthorn give way to pedestrian promenades, to a built environment punctuated by public arts works, such as Rob Conybear's Lighthouse Tower at the junction of Ocean Crescent and Maritime Walk. Rob's quirky work looks as if a ferocious wind has blown bits of scrap metal which have then glued themselves onto the lighthouse lamp on its column of Portland stone. It's a bit like Heath Robinson after a whirlwind, but it does raise a broad smile.

The walkway here celebrates some of the barques and ships that sailed from here round Cape Horn, such as *Galatea, Mohican* and *Ocean Rover*. The Sail Bridge, crossing the Tawe, was designed by the same architectural firm who created the bridge that fans across the Tyne in Gateshead. It was the shape of things to come as new marina berths and swanky eateries extended chichi Swansea eastwards and Fabian Way changed from express way to espresso way.

The grand sweep of Swansea Bay always delights the eye and it's well worth the heart-pounding climb up Constitution Hill to revel in it. Unless you're able to grow wings, take a flask of oxygen as it's a steeply raked gradient that would make Sherpa Tensing pant. Halfway up, there's a handrail, for when you begin to feel ancient and creaky – unless you're in peak, Olympic condition, of course.

At the top, take as many deep breaths as you can, steady the blood. The curve of Mumbles Head, with its lifeboat station and lighthouse, makes for the main focal point, but the mudflats of Blackpill and out towards Oystermouth are also a sublime register of change, of the state of the tide, the reflections and refractions producing sheen and shimmer; the shirr of small waves over sand and shallows coruscating the light, glinting it, setting out fields of tiny seashore diamonds.

The canvas of sky above the water is a great place to cloud watch, from pewter cumulus bringing in galoshes-weather to candy floss whispers of cirrus, high up. It's a cliché to say it's an ever-changing panorama, so let's say it changes wondrously, a quotidian delight for all who climb up here.

A writer for the *Gloucester Journal* in 1786 compared Swansea with Brighton and early travellers to the town found it a delight, although the changes wrought by industry would later make it resemble one of the seven circles of hell, wreathed in sulphurous clouds. Those have long dissipated.

Unlike Cardiff, which severed most of its connection with the sea by building a barrage, Swansea remains a city with a real maritime connection. The air along the marina is ozone-charged and has the tang of laver bread about it, the scent of far-off deep ocean. It has the former dockside warehouse now converted into the National Waterfront Museum. Inside there is ample testimony to the fact that Swansea was both a powerhouse and dynamo during the Industrial Revolution, even if it meant sitting under toxic cloud fields.

Swansea was simply one of the most important places in the whole of Wales's Copper Kingdom, with the ore mined from Parys Mountain on Anglesey and transported to the Tawe for smelting. Sailors from Swansea had great reputations for traversing the seven seas, facing perils and waves as big as cathedrals. And when they got to far away ports in countries such as Chile they pined for home and the women they had left behind and rendered that homesickness in the form of shanties…

So take me ropes and make me fast,
In ol' Swansea Town once more!
Now we're outward bound around Cape Horn,
To 'Frisco and around,
I'll send you letters when we get there, an' you'll know
I'm homeward bound ol' gal.

But they sent more than letters. Mariners would paint images of foreign harbours on feathers and post them back in lieu of cards. Feather postcards! They have some at the Glynn Vivian art gallery, itself a legacy of the copper bonanza, as it was founded by one of the sons of Swansea's biggest copper-owners.

A crow hop away, the names of the yachts and speedboats at anchor in the 550-berth marina give one a glimpse of the dreams and aspiration of middle-aged men. There are the soft spots for animals – *Ocelot, Greyhound* and *Cadno* – and for avifauna – *Cormorant, Osprey, Sea Hawk, Blue Jay, Kingfisher* and *Gwylan;* but then there's the exotica, named like lap dancers – *Lounei, Azzurra, Iolanthe, San-Won, Aztec* and *Antares*. Then there are the craft named after wives, or mistresses – *Rhiannon, Jessica Anne* and *Manon,* and others that reflect on life and its stages – *My Mid Life Crisis, Wet Dream* and *Indian Summer*.

Beyond Mumbles lies Gower, a peninsula lying between two rivers, namely the Llwchwr and the Tawe – with the hump of Cefn Bryn as its brackeny backbone. Gower was the very first Area of Outstanding Beauty designated in the UK. And it is beautiful. Intimate, time-trapped villages. Pastoral landscapes of burnt gorse and hardy wild ponies, purple foxglove, basking

adders and exulting skylarks. Occasionally you might hear what the poet Nigel Jenkins enchantingly describes as the 'sorcelling song of the curlew.'

In the main, Gower is made out of limestone, with its central ridge composed of old red sandstone, its southern rim is wind-whittled and tide-engraved to create charm-filled bays: the peninsula as a whole has nineteen of them, places such as Langland with its bobbing forms of rubberized surfer dudes in white catspaws of swell; Caswell with its grand hotel and then, the pebbly and picturesque bay at Pwll Du. Here a stream of eponymous black water is corralled and lagooned behind a sea shingle bank. Tuning in to the rhythmic shush of waves against

shiny rock, it is hard to imagine this place as a seat of industry, yet it was one of the busiest quarries hereabouts, employing as many as 200 men in its early 19th-century heyday. Walk around the coast of Wales and there are ghosts of so many industries, blowing away like puffball dust.

Some of these coves are impossibly charming tourist traps, such as the hugely photogenic Three Cliffs, snapped by all, and Gower's most southerly point, Port Eynon – where salt was manufactured and oysters gathered: each one backdropped by cliffs.

The further you get away from Swansea, the less the effect of bungalow blight and the more you enter well tended land, with flavourful potatoes and cauliflowers with huge white hearts, and

Three Cliffs Bay

villages with history in their names. The Normans settled the south of Gower, importing immigrants with their language and ways.

If you like a good reed bed then Oxwich is the place to go: it's an evocative habitat, bringing to mind the poems of Yeats especially when the wind through the high stands of Phragmites sounds like a stately banshee. The National Nature Reserve here covers, and protects, much of the area of Oxwich Bay, one of the richest varieties of coastal habitat in Britain. The foreshore, dunes, marshes and woodlands hold an abundance of species, with no fewer than 600 flowering plants. Some species at Oxwich are a little more spectral. The churchyard of St Illtyd's is reputedly haunted, and the *ceffyl dŵr*, or water horse, has been sighted here, visiting in secret to drink out of the sacred well.

It's well worth the climb 'n' scramble to get to Paviland cave. Here you can get not only a sense of history, but of prehistory. There can be few caves as remarkable as this one, known as the Goat's Hole, where one can imagine what life was like in the Ice Age, when the glaciers slowly retreated. Here 29,000 years ago Stone Age men brought one of their own to be buried. The body was laid to rest next to the skull of an adult mammoth and was buried wearing red ochre-stained funeral clothes, which gave rise to the popular name for this skeleton, namely the Red Lady of Paviland, that was until they realized it was the remains of a young man. But the name sort of stuck.

William Buckland, the first ever Professor of Geology at Oxford University was the official discoverer of the skeleton. He had arrived at Goat's Hole on the 18th of January, 1823, to begin an exploration, tipped off by the family who lived in nearby Penrice Castle.

After scrambling along to the cave, you can imagine a time when the sea was a very distant prospect and the plain in front of you was roamed by a menagerie of animals. Armour-plated rhinos would have grazed the grasslands of this South Wales Serengeti, not to mention a plenitude of deer stalked by that

Last resting place at Rhossili

designer carnivore, the sabre-toothed tiger, while hyenas would startle the nights with their wild cries. The cave was a refuge from all this, although visiting bears could still unsettle any sheltering humans.

Because of the soluble nature of the rocks of south Gower they are often honeycombed with such caves, like the ones at Rhossili. Offshore, Worm's Head takes its name from Vikings who thought it looked like a dragon. It still does.

The northern coast of Gower has a very different character to the south, with great acres of salt marsh, including Whiteford Burrows, with its long beach and lighthouse. The mossified silence of the pine woodland leads onto the earthwork dyke and dune edge of The Groose, leading to where The Great Pill opens out, sinewing into the channels of Landimore marsh, with its wild horses and soul-enriching emptiness.

Here stands the only cast-iron lighthouse to be built on the British seaside. It was erected in 1865 to safeguard increased trade in and out of Llanelli and Burry Port, the other side of the Llwchwr. The base of it is a perfect place to scan the waves for eider duck, the only resident flock in Wales. They are the heavi-

est British ducks but when they fly they are determined flyers, indeed the fastest species of bird in level flight.

Further out, brent geese, diminutive and perpetually busy, work the beds of zostera, a tasty eel grass which they favour over all other marine breakfasts. A small grebe – Slavonian or black headed, it's too far way to say for certain – plops underwater and rises far enough away to be almost out of sight. Curlews probe muddy margins, their long down-curved bills probing the slime for a richness of ragworms, lugworms, and other invertebrates to needle out of the shallows. And there are oystercatchers, black and white tuxedoed ranks of them. Calling together, they are an Andean pipe band warming up, a winter symphony among the Spartina grass.

When I was a boy, they had a cull of these black-and-white waders, with their satsuma orange bills, as they were blamed for the diminishing stocks of cockles. Men with shotguns blasted away freely. Nowadays man takes the brunt of the blame, emptying all manner of pollutants which gather in these filtering animals.

On the way back to Cwm Ivy, an early barn owl ghosts along a line of wire, its golden wings bronzed by the westering sun. It floats in the chill air, its vole detectors on orange alert, its feathery talons slightly agape in anticipation.

Further down the coast stands the village of Penclawdd, forever synonymous with the cockle women who worked the sandy beds out in the Llwchwr. Their donkeys would be laden with bags of shellfish, which they would prepare and sell around the houses, baskets on their heads. The marshes are empty now, other than for wheeling drifts of black-headed gulls which shriek maniacally every now and then, tossed on the wild air like scraps of white tissue paper.

We're now on the other side of the Llwchwr, the northern edge of the Burry estuary. Llanelli has the most transformed

Culver Hole, Port Eynon

stretch of coast in Wales. Steelworks, copperworks, brickworks and iron foundries commandeered huge swathes of land on reclaimed marshlands here, not to mention the slag and other side-products which built up over the years. The sound of works' hooters punctuated my childhood. But following the decline in heavy industry came nothing short of total transformation. Where once foundries flared the night sky, turning it into perpetual sunset, and chimney stacks rose like birch thickets, the shoreline is now the busy preserve of legions of cyclists and walkers. No fewer than two thousand acres of former industrial land became the Millennium Coastal Park, allowing a post-industrial town to enter the leisure age. Machynys, which used to be all heavy metal foundries is now faux Cape Cod housing, with fine dining at the golf club – delicacies such as Avruga caviar, smoked salmon with blinis and frozen lemon vodka.

The Millennium Coastal Park has reclaimed, sculpted and generally opened up land previously locked away behind factory gates and now you can enjoy the coastline all the way from Loughor Bridge to the Pembrey saltings – cycle it, amble along it, or even whizz along the tarmacadam paths by skateboard.

Mark Newton appreciates such paths. He recently completed a circuit of the entire Welsh coast on his mobility scooter. 'I knackered my leg in the army in 1991, it was dislocated during PT and put back in place badly.' He then got septicaemia in his knee which was subsequently supplanted by arthritis.

On a good day Mark, who was brought up on the edge of the Llwchwr, would be able to cover thirty miles in a day, even if the rigours of the terrain sorely tested his vehicle, especially on slopes such as Dinas Head near Fishguard: little wonder the motor burned out near New Quay.

There were days he was pretty much alone in the landscape for he didn't encounter many people in Pembrokeshire and found Broad Haven pretty empty. But there was always plenty to see. He thinks that wildlife is less wary of a man on a scooter

Mark Newton at Mwnt, Ceredigion

and indeed he conducts surveys of little ringed plover for the Countryside Council for Wales on his. Not that wildlife was always benign: as he recalls: 'I had my food nicked by badgers one night at Trearddur Bay...'

As he scootered the Welsh coast, the former squaddie in the 1st The Queen's Dragoon Guards, or the Welsh Cavalry, saw some sights he will always treasure. He'd not been to Llŷn before and loved 'the gorgeous view of Bardsey from the coastguard look-out at Uwchmynydd.' Mark also enjoyed getting up close to auks such as guillemots and puffins at South Stack and delighted in porpoise watching at Point Lynas on Anglesey. He thrilled to the sight of fifty bottlenose dolphins at New Quay. Undaunted by the up-and-down nature of the Welsh coast, Mark now has his sights sets on scootering the entire coast of Britain.

The National Wetlands Centre at Penclacwydd is a sort of Welsh Slimbridge, with captive wildfowl such as the Hawaiian ne-ne and snow geese prettying the lagoons around the visitor centre, as well as their free flight cousins which visit the reedy expanses and areas of standing water in the nature reserve. They've clocked up two hundred species, from the mega-rare

Richard's pipit, long-billed dowitcher and red-footed falcon to great congregations of commoner birds which gather here in great number. There are non-avian species too, such as the ever hungry water vole, popularly known as the water rat, able to scoff eighty per cent of its own body weight each day; and rare trees too, such as the black poplar which likes to send down robust roots in waterlogged places.

The sluggish, muddy flow of the river Lliedi doesn't seem to be enough of a flow to scour Llanelli docks clean as it did in the town's industrial heyday. Nowadays the area is identikit marina, with many flats occupied by members of the town's new Polish community. Out on the sands, human cockle gatherers work at low tide, their four-wheel-drive vehicles ready for a quick geta-way before the waters rise.

Then on past Pwll, where I grew up. The lakes here were meant to become a mecca for coarse fishermen but someone mis-calculated the effects of high tides and all the freshwater fish that had been stocked were killed. It's a village which has had its connection with the sea severed by the main line railway. As a schoolboy, I once spotted the fact that the sea wall had been washed away and saved a train from being wrecked. British Rail gave me a hardback copy of *The Collins Guide to British Birds* as a reward for my heroism. I have it still.

Even though the main line cut off the village from the estuary, that didn't stop characters such as Clocsi catching fish in an unorthodox way. He would walk across the estuary at low tide having driven iron nails through the wooden soles of his clogs, spearing flat fish such as dabs simply by walking over them.

One of the sunniest memories of growing up here was of gathering cockles on Pwll beach for tea. Villagers said you should wait three tides before eating the ones in the bucket. They were right. Sprinkled with malt vinegar and white pepper they made a meal fit for a prince – of Atlantis.

Firing range, Laugharne

Walking on west, past Richard Harries's enormous earthwork 'The Wave' and Burry Port is the next, well, port of call. It's hard to conjure up this place in its heyday when tonnes of coal and tinplate were shipped out. Now it's all pleasure craft such as *Niwl y Môr, Sailfish* and the wonderfully named *Plan B*.

Cefn Sidan, the beach that extends from Pembrey, right along to the muddy mouth of the Gwendraeth estuary to the west, is a place where one can find an uncommon solitude.

Seven miles long, Cefn Sidan, which translates as silky back, can be as smooth as silk and as dangerous, like a stocking turned into a garrotte. This stretch of wild coast has seen many a shipwreck, with no fewer than 182 vessels grounded on the beach since the 1600s, carrying cargo ranging from seal skins to juniper berries, buffalo hides to rum. A recent beaching was a yacht from Morocco carrying a huge cargo of cannabis. That mind-altering flotsam attracted many an optimistic hippie beachcomber.

Not every historical wreck was an accident: local people were said to light false beacons to lure ships in, and their macabre habit of carrying weapons with them, led to these land-based pirates being known as *gwŷr y bwyelli bach*, the men with the little hatchets.

It's also a beach that sees many other objects washed ashore. It has more cetacean beachings – whales and dolphins – than anywhere else in Wales. They even had a walrus washed up back in 1986, while sometimes millions of sailor-by-the-wind jellyfish are stranded on the shore. One day the whole strandline turned orange after the wreck of a ship carrying Hawaiian Tropic Sun Tan lotion. Not much use in Llanelli, where rainfall is pretty constant.

In the surf offshore, numerous common scoter, charcoal-black sea ducks, fish in defiance of all the wild churn and whipping spume. Carmarthen Bay is an important wintering ground for them, with plentiful shellfish secreted in the sand beneath the waves. Theirs is a challenging habitat, but they're up to the challenge, scything through the chill water, bobbing to the surface like blackened corks.

Winter is a good time to come here, not only because of the guarantee of hermitic peace – if you can filter out the constant sibilance of sou'westerlies – but because of the constant presence of sanderlings, those silvery-plumaged wading birds that run like clockwork along the frothy edge of spindrift, their legs moving with Swiss precision, delicate and determined. Rounding the shingle spit of Tywyn Point you're entering a bombing range. I know this for a fact. I was crossing it one day when the RAF started target practice, the shells tearing up the ground around me. Scary day, that.

But then enter the entirely overlooked and neglected glories of the Gwendraeth estuary. The salt marshes, dissected and bifurcated by creeks, are good places to watch fifteen-spined sticklebacks sharking in shoals through the shallows.

For fans of mellifluous alliteration, it gets no better than Laugharne, with its connections with Dylan Thomas, the boozy, cherub-faced bard whose 'house on stilts' overlooks the 'heron priested shore' of the Taf estuary, while the poet's remains are interred in the churchyard. His working shed is preserved, complete with fag-butt-strewn floor, and it's easy to imagine him here, rhyming and hymning a euphonious world into glorious being.

Pendine has a faster pace, occasionally. Its long beach has been a testing ground for fast cars, and in the 1920s the Welsh TT motorbike races were held on its sandy flats. Some speed kings have met their deaths here. J.G. Parry Thomas, in his car called Babs, died during a land speed record attempt in 1927 at an estimated 170 miles per hour. With that in mind I drive away at 30 miles per hour, one careful driver.

Dylan Thomas's writing shed

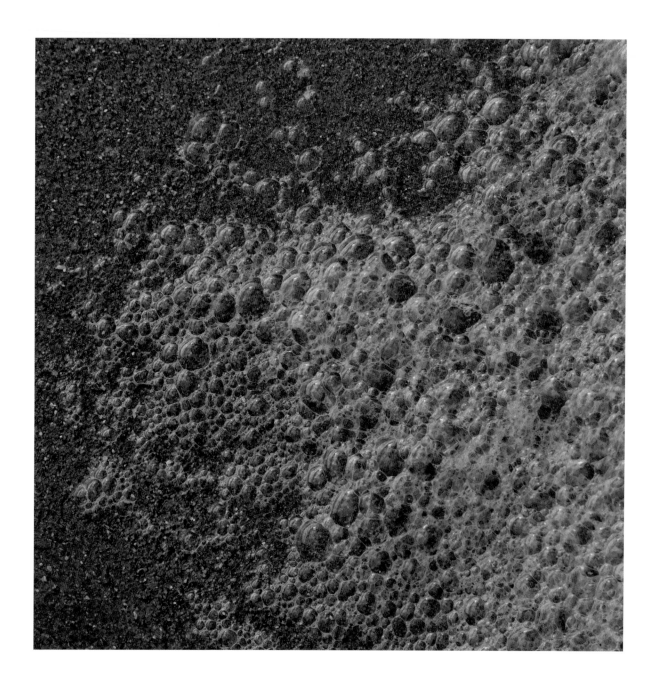

Fall Bay, Gower

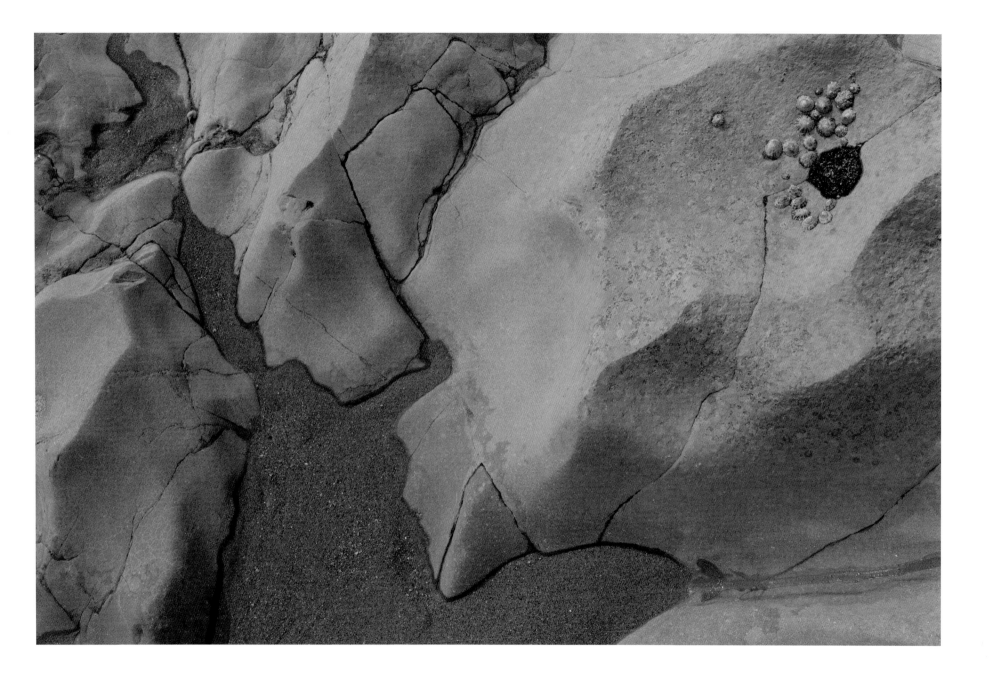

Mewslade Bay, Gower

Whiteford Point, Gower

Worm's Head, Gower

3 **Amroth to Skomer**
Sand Churches
on the Beach

Bullslaughter Bay

The great sweep of storm-washed, pebble and sandy beach at Amroth marks the beginning of the Pembrokeshire Coast Path, born amidst the spirit of optimism that followed the Second World War. The National Park, of which it is perhaps the most visible aspect, was designated in 1952. The Path took a while to create, mainly because of the many different landowners along its route, but now it's both tourist magnet and beautiful resource.

It was the veteran naturalist R.M. Lockley who first mapped out the coastal path in the early 1950s, which involved negotiations with 150 landowners, which called for great powers of diplomacy. Rights of way were steadily negotiated and bargained for. It took until 1970 to open it officially, but then there is such a thing as Pembrokeshire time, which allows one to watch the

Tideline debris, Bullslaugher Bay

hands of the clock moving. No rush. The Park was designated, in part, because of the near complete range of geological features encountered on the 300-kilometre, or 186-mile, hike from here to the path's other end in St Dogmaels.

Pembrokeshire does possess an incredibly various coast – eroded into Gaudi cathedrals of rock and sea-thrifted headlands, unscalable promontories and sandy beaches, splintered rocks and pebble ridges, all part of an elegant and very slow dance to the music of time, as continents shift and collide and the wind gouges and the waves erode. For even the land beneath you is slowly, ever so slowly, moving even as you stand stock still. Stand for a moment on the beach at Amroth and imagine a time when you were much nearer the equator – almost on it – and even now you're moving imperceptibly slowly towards Scandinavia. And more recent history has its surprises, too: it's easy to forget that many of the houses in the village were built to house coal miners, or indeed that there was a coal industry here in Pembrokeshire, on the outermost western limits of the South Wales coalfield, even if the black stuff is separated from the main bulk of anthracite and soft coal further east.

If the tide is sufficiently low, you can see the remains of a petrified forest, blackened ancient tree stumps reaching up from the mud, part-fossilized remnants of the woodlands that would have flourished following the last Ice Age. It's believed by archaeologists that the forest would have been destroyed by inundation when the sea levels rose about 7,000 years ago.

Stretch your wings, soar effortlessly like a fulmar, hugging the coast, over Coppet Hall Point, Wiseman's Bridge and on past Saundersfoot and its charter boats, like the *Happy Hooker*, specialising in catching tope and porbeagle sharks. Let the wind lift and veer, over Trevay Farm and Monkstone Point and then let your eyes alight on picture postcard perfection... *Croeso i Ddinbych y Pysgod*. Welcome to Tenby. As beautiful as St Ives, only less Cornish.

Tenby

I first went to Tenby when I was five, on a Sunday school trip from Libanus chapel in Pwll. Before the bus took us there, we children imagined candy floss clouds and a lighthouse made of seaside rock, yet even now, when I know those skies are likely to be leaden with Welsh rain, and it has no lighthouse worth the name, the place still exerts a definite magic.

One pictures the town in the mind's eye as an elderly dowager, slowly pulling on long white gloves and wearing her best jewellery, knowing she can still make an impression. It's a town shot through with an elegant stateliness, not to mention a fine amalgam of architectures. The lovely pastels of the Georgian houses – limeade through teal to terracotta – the charmscape of the harbour complete with silvery tinkle from the boat rigging, all make up the weft and weave of that magic. Away from the chattery crowds along High Street and Lower Frog Street, and the thinnest possible mist of monosaturate fats floating from the fryers of cod-and-chips emporia, the very substantial church of St Mary's is well worth a gander. There are architectural borrowings from the West Country and on one side of the nave is a memorial to Robert Recorde, the pioneering mathematician who first started to discuss maths in English, not Greek, who also invented the equals sign, or Tenby = tourist heaven.

Taking the air on the esplanade gives the visitor fine views of Caldey or Ynys Bŷr, still home to monks and their devotions, not to mention an aptitude for making lavender scent. It's a blessed bee that happens to make landfall on the island.

You expect much from a place vaunted as 'the most pleasant place in Wales.' That's how Gerald of Wales, Giraldus Cambrensis, described Manorbier castle, halfway between Tenby and Pembroke. Then again our earliest travel writer was biased. The author of the ebullient 12th-century *Journey Around Wales* was brought up here, famously building sand churches on the beach while his brothers were erecting sand castles. This was, after all a boy who wanted to be a bishop when he grew up, to leave behind his pleasant home with its clement days of childhood and its carp ponds, while his brothers wanted to be soldiers.

But it's blustery when I get there, with a December-edged wind flailing through a May day and fluting wildly through the castle arrow slits.

Beyond the grey shingle of beach, diehard surfers look like fly-specks against great panes of sea, as west coast tsunamis curl in and try to wipe them away. As the rain sheets in, I envy the wave-riders their rubberized suits, but would happily make do with some old fashioned oilcloth, like my grandfather's fishing coat, with pockets deep enough for a dozen sea bass. The wind if anything accelerates. A defiant surfer crests a wave as if he's in Santa Cruz, teetering on the white, spuming edge. Soon I'm as wet as a frog.

A large swathe of the Castlemartin peninsula is given over to military use, so red warning flags keep the public away from the tank training area and hazards of unexploded artillery shells as soldiers prepare for Afghanistan and other war theatres. Then, on the north western rim of the peninsula there are other kinds of tanks, oil tanks and refinery stacks which surround the now deserted village of Rhoscrowther, its denizens cleared out to make way for Texaco in the early 1960s. But there are more peaceful and less sullied spots out on the peninsula, not least the church of St Govan's, wedged into a cleft in the rock, and the tranquillity of Bosherston pools, one of the country's more reliable places to see otter families gambolling among the lily pads.

One of Wales's most interesting artists lived in the village of Castlemartin. Arthur Giardelli made complicated works of art using watchsprings and seashells, which he gathered at nearby beaches such as Freshwater West. The clock mechanisms acted as a commentary on the way the shells accrete and take shape over time, while the shells reminded one of the fact that nature's timetable is quite unlike our own, measured out in a pitiful three score years and ten. And all shaped by a blind watchmaker...

Then there's geological time, measured out in millennia and legendary time, which is simply unmeasurable. The deep waterway at Milford Haven, in places as deep as 18 metres, is a drowned valley, or ria, and is old enough to have been visited by the legendary King Arthur, according, at least, to the tale of Culhwch and Olwen in the Mabinogi.

It is a little more certain that Lord Nelson visited in 1802 when he was of the opinion that here was a waterway second only to Trincomalee in Ceylon. The tidal waters of the river Cleddau extend 30 km inland from its mouth, reaching as far as the county town of Haverfordwest, and the coast along the river reaches is studded with jetties, quays and landing places. Its per-ceived military importance led to the fortification of the harbour and the creation of a dozen forts and Martello towers to defend it, including the very substantial fort at Scoveston, covering the approaches to Neyland. All of this building work was collectively part of an enormous knee-jerk reaction to a threat of French inva-sion, and these defences are therefore collectively known as Palmerston's Follies, after the Prime Minister of the time, Lord Palmerston. Yet although men such as Lord Hamilton played a role in the creation of the town of Milford Haven – he was the man authorized by an 1790 Act of Parliament to build 'Quays, Docks, Piers and other Erections' – it owes its true genesis in great meas-ure to his nephew and to the British government's desire at the turn of the 19th century to develop a whale fishery in the world's southern oceans. Yes, whales.

After a successful marketing campaign, Lord Hamilton's nephew, Sir Charles Greville attracted New England whaling fam-ilies such as the Starbucks and the Folgers to settle on the Haven from their new base in Dartmouth, Nova Scotia. The Nantucketers had settled there as a result of their businesses being disrupted,

or seeing their ships destroyed, by the American Revolutionary War in 1783. In Britain taxes on whale oil were prohibitively high and it made sense to locate here, as it was then the main market.

The plan was to build docks, quays and a Quaker meeting house by the time the families arrived, but these did not transpire, yet at least fifteen Nantucket whale men and their families came to Milford in 1792. Their ships were big, built to withstand raging oceans and weighing anything up to 350 tonnes.

The history of these early settlers of the town is still recorded in street names such as Starbuck Road. The fact that the Starbucks opened a bakery in the town hints at what was to come when members of the extended family started to sell coffee as well!

But nowadays it's not whale oil that dominates the Haven. It's Chevron, Murco, Captain and Doba crude, not to mention a new energy source, liquefied natural gas, harvested elsewhere and brought in by ship. But oil and nature-rich waters don't mix, as evidenced by the *Sea Empress* disaster. This traumatic event occurred on the 15th of February, 1996, when the 140,000-tonne oil tanker went aground on rocks at the entrance to Milford Haven. Over the next six days, an estimated 72,000 tonnes of

Oiled seabirds, Freshwater East, February 1996

Forties Blend crude oil and 360 tonnes of heavy fuel oil were spilled into the sea and contaminated over one hundred kilometres of the Pembrokeshire coast. The sight of seabirds wrapped in a toxic sludge of oil was a stark reminder of the dangers of so much heavy oil shipping in environmentally rich, and therefore sensitive areas. And some of those lie just offshore.

One of the jewels in the Pembrokeshire crown is Skokholm island, a wooded isle according to the Vikings, though there's precious little trace of woodland on its old red sandstone nowadays. The island was home to Britain's first bird observatory, established there by R.M. Lockley in 1933.

As with many of the Welsh islands, it's worth staying over-night: in the case of Skokholm to venture down to the old quarry in the lee of the lighthouse, to search for a tiny bird of deep ocean.

The storm petrel is Britain's smallest seabird. Although it is smaller than a house sparrow, it is tough and resilient, a truly pelagic species that spends almost all of its life at sea. Not being a strong flyer, storms may blow the bird inland and explains why it has been known traditionally as a symbol of bad weather, with 'wrecks' of these birds often seen at river mouths and even inland after gales and hurricanes. Yet, this doesn't happen all that often: it takes a tempest and a half to get the better of these hardy oceanic birds. They are adept at seeking shelter by keeping to the troughs of the waves and avoiding the crests.

Milford Haven

On calm days the storm petrel, also known to sailors as Mother Carey's chicken, will patter over the surface of the water as if it is walking – the very name 'petrel' is said to be derived from the Biblical episode in which St Peter walked on the water. This graceful facility is achieved by the bird making concentrated, delicate wing-beats, just enough to keep it airborne. Its feet are seen to dangle and touch the surf as it looks for traces of food. This behaviour is typically seen when large groups of birds trail behind ships such as trawlers, where the disturbed water can reveal tasty morsels, which they pick at in the same way as blue tits visiting bird feeders.

In the walls and quarry of Skokholm it is possible to hear the purring 'song' of the petrels, safe in their tiny underground burrows, crooning their location-finder hymns to the night. But this isn't the only wildlife island in these waters.

As the May or June afternoon wears on on Skomer island, the puffins return to stand outside their nesting burrows and they can be trustingly tame: you can walk across the springy cliff-top turf and get within feet, sometimes inches of one. Its bright coloration is that of the clown, as is the forlorn look and pattern of sadness about the eyes. The puffin's bill is bright, triangular, and a very useful tool, for attracting a mate, for excavating a burrow, for sparring with other puffins over territory (a couple of birds might lock bills and tumble hundreds of yards down a cliff in

St Anne's Head from Blockhouse West

determined scuffle) and for catching fish. You might see a single bird carry back as many as ten sand eels in its bill. This species of auk has backward-pointing spines on its tongue and the roof of its mouth which it employs during each dive to scoop up and hold as many fish as possible.

The birds whirr down to the water, their wings beating 400 times a minute, yet it's underwater that these supreme swimmers come into their own. Aeronautically they might not seem well designed, but underwater they are aquanautically adept, twisting and depth-charging after sand eels, flashing silver shoals of them, which aren't easy prey.

But the island comes astonishingly to life at night. At North Haven on Skomer the Manx shearwaters start their late night caterwauling, making that blood-curdling, or possibly blood-gargling cry. R.M.Lockley described it as being like the sound of a rooster in full cry seconds after its throat has been cut. In Pembrokeshire these shearwaters are called cocklollies, an onomatopeic attempt to capture the essence of their cries in the night.

Eerie and mysterious as the Manxie's cry undoubtedly is, it's still one of my favourite sounds in nature and Chris Taylor agrees with me. He's the warden here and you can see the delight in his eyes even at two in the morning, when the firmament is ablaze with stars, which compete with the lights of tankers lined up in a stately row waiting to discharge at the Milford Haven refineries.

This is Chris's second season and he's planning on staying here for a good few years. He knows that it will be time to leave should he ever refer to the place as *his* island, when in fact it's a place for puffins tame enough to stroll past your boots, a consequence of their never having been hunted here, unlike say Anglesey where they have recipes for these comedic birds.

Chris has a Gloucestershire laugh as ripe as exploding fruit and talks with abundant love about Skomer, as he explains that its Viking name means cloven isle. He has also done his sums: on its cliffs and banks nest 300,000 birds, from the guillemots in serried ranks on ledges, to the shearwaters in their burrows, and the popular puffins. Earlier in the evening there were veritable flurries of them whirring onto the cliffs, the lucky ones carrying tiny silver ribbons. But now the island belongs to the shearwaters, which crash through the bracken as they home in on their burrows.

These birds nest off the Welsh coast but overwinter off the coast of Argentina, Brazil and Uruguay, flying in a great migratory loop that takes them past west Africa before scything across the South Atlantic. For they are astonishing flyers, shearing the waves like mini-albatrosses, and because of their incredible annual migrations, a reminder that they are an international responsibility of ours.

Two or three Manx shearwaters fly past the white orb of the moon. It is a sight of ineffable and humbling beauty. Time to sleep, as a tangerine sliver of light is already widening on the eastern horizon. Day and night are married here.

Chris Taylor, warden of Skomer Island

A Skomer puffin

Church Doors, Skrinkle Haven

Skokholm Island

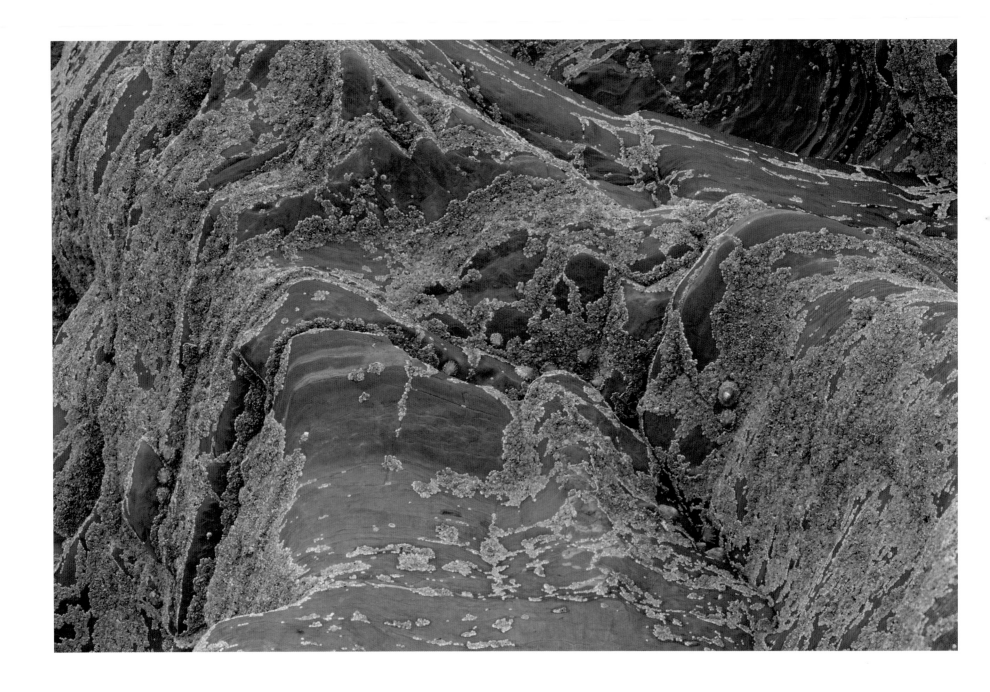

Presipe, near Manorbier

Skomer Island

4 **Skomer to Teifi**
Of Gales and Mermaids and Ancient Stones

Strumble Head

The southernmost waves of St Bride's Bay wash Marloes Head, which curves out to sea south of Little Haven as if to fingerpost Skomer island. Meanwhile, depending on the weather, its northern waves crash or caress Penmaen Dewi, or St David's Head. Between these two arms lies a fairly low coastline punctuated by havens – Little, Broad, Druidston, Madoc's and Nolton Haven – although nowadays one of the bay's most distinctive features is the preponderance of outsized oil tankers at anchor, waiting their turn to disgorge at that other haven, Milford.

Newgale is one of the most dramatic stretches of coast, an operatic stretch of coast even, a great gusting aria which tells of gales and mermaids and ancient stones, and sung with a gusto that tosses the very clouds hither and thither. The stage-set is a pebble beach and a half, a storm tossed sea-bank that can hold back hurricane riptides and tame wildcat tempests when they're thrown onshore from the Celtic Deeps. Most of the time.

Newgale is poised on more than one boundary. It's clearly set between land and sea but it also sits astride the Landsker, the linguistic dividing line that separates the English-speaking lands of South Pembrokeshire's Little England, where Flemish settlers were brought in by the Normans, from the Welsh-speaking north of the county.

In the Duke of Edinburgh pub I met a lovely man, retired teacher Roy Watkins, who moved to the village in 1965. He was nursing a lunchtime pint of Guinness poured by a steady hand. Roy is the only Welsh speaker in Newgale and it occurs to me that he is the Landsker, the living embodiment of this linguistic divide. After his days the line will retreat northwards.

He invites me to visit the garden of his bungalow, indubitably the one with the best, most expansive view of the three-mile-long Newgale beach and behind it the grey length of pebble protection that ensures that low lying parts of the village don't turn into an aquarium. Yet the sea has broken through, most recently in 1989. Roy remembers it well, and how the waves exerted their fearful majesty: 'You wouldn't believe the force of the sea as it followed the course of the river. It lifted a garage into the air and took away the side of the café.' A police car was scooped up by the waves and turned over several times, only to land on its wheels again, with the blue light on the roof still flashing.

Gerald of Wales describes a historical precedent for this:

> The wind blew with such unprecedented violence that the
> shores of south Wales were completely denuded of sand…
> The tempest raged so fiercely that conger-eels and many
> other sea-fish were driven up on the high rocks and
> into the bushes by the force of the wind and the men
> came to gather them.

When you find yourself fishing on the hedges in the morning, picking cod off the hawthorn, you know that you've seen some bad weather.

In Newgale, the sea level is rising centimetre by centimetre with every passing year and some anticipate the day when they might lose the main road and have to abandon the pub, the shop and the camping site for ever. Which might explain why Roy is going back for another pint of velvet at the Duke that evening. He might as well while it's still there.

It delights the eye. The river Solva, today the intense colour of Chartreuse, winds leisurely into the sea through a beautiful natural harbour, protected from storm surge by the windbreaker headlands of Gewni and Penrhyn.

Now the domain of Sunday sailors and leisure craft, Solva was once a veritable hive of maritime activity. In the 19th century there were 36 local boats at anchor here, trading wood, lime and

Newgale

Linda Evans and her father, Wyn, at Caerfai

butter, among other commodities and goods. There were other less legitimate transactions, too. Ship wreckers thrived on the cargoes of boats lured onto rocks such as Green Scar, Black Scar and the Mare: one of the techniques used hereabouts was to tie a lantern to the tail of a cow and let it swing after the animal. It's a good story, if a little beefed up. Legend also has it that a local vicar used to pray using the words 'please send us a shipwreck and, please, may we be the first to get there.' After a wreck, villagers would swarm out of their houses, intent on plunder, stripping the clothes of the dead and even cutting off fingers to rob, then sequester, gold rings. The booty would be stored in clandestine cupboards in their houses, making it a wary, secretive village. Nowadays it's a place for city folk to visit their second homes, picturesque and pretty vacant for much of the year.

Caerfai farm, on the southern rim of the St David's peninsula, overlooks the small sandy Caerfai Bay and beyond that the sweep of St Bride's Bay. The farmer at Caerfai, Wyn Evans, isn't just a livestock farmer, he farms energy. Thirty years ago he was a pioneer, seen by some, of course, as an eccentric for deciding to turn farm waste into a resource, and a valuable source of energy to boot: 'We're not only farming the land but we're farming the resources that pass over the land. If you can produce your food using the least amount of fossil fuel, it's better for everybody. People say I'm only saving peanuts but if you save enough of them you'll have a sackful.'

In his way he's also saving the world. Cow slurry produces methane, or biogas, which is twenty times more damaging to the environment than CO_2. On this farm the cow waste is gathered in a tank under the milking parlour. Then it's diluted and pumped into a holding tank and thence into a home-made digester where the gas is generated, passes down a pipe and into a gas holder. The gas is then combusted and the energy used to heat a water tank and even a cooking stove. It's used to make cheese among other things. This is a highly diversified farm as well as being eco-friendly. Even the by-product of the biogas process is useful. The digestate, or digested slurry, is a very good, organic fertilizer that can protect against soil compaction and erosion and is mega high in nutrients. It feeds the soil to grow the grass to feed the cows who make the poo and the whole grand cycle is repeated.

Wyn has also equipped the farm with photovoltaic panels on the roofs which allow him so sell surplus power back to the National Grid. He's also got a ground source heat exchange, involving a metal coil set in the ground, to extract heat from the earth and, as one might expect, a simple wind turbine. Between them these renewable sources can produce half of the farm's energy needs. Wyn's daughter, Linda, makes cheese and the power used is all homegrown, or generated.

There have been many changes in the natural environment in the years Wyn has been farming at Caerfai: 'Snow blizzards used to be a real problem in this area. I can remember when my third daughter was born in February 1978 and the blizzard was that bad that there was no way of getting my wife to the hospital in Haverfordwest, so there was no choice but to have a home birth. In contrast, one recent February day we had our four grandchildren here all with their shirts off and paddling in the paddling pool and down on the beach – that was how warm it was. That's just happened in the last thirty years.'

The sea is very much a part of Wyn's life and he's looking at it all the time: this explains what he's trying to do: 'Once we get sea level rise, we get tremendous amount of erosion and people having to leave coastal cities. That's why I do what I do. Back in 1999 our first grandchildren came along and I didn't want their grandchildren coming along and saying that I knew about climate change and was in a position to do something and didn't. I don't want them to say, what did he do?'

The next bay along to Caerfai is St Non's Bay, named after the mother of Wales's patron saint, St David. On the rocks of Pen y Cyfrwy, bottle-green shags stand sleek and sentinel, their feathers outstretched to dry in a salty wind. As the coastal path winds round the headlands towards St David's with its architectural grandeur, it's good to pause at the ruinous chapel dedicated to Non. This marks the spot where she gave birth – in the middle of a fearful storm, of course – to the Welsh patron saint, having been raped by Sanctus the king of Ceredigion. But that's just myth, or very, very old gossip.

Facts are understandably as rare as roseate terns when it comes to Non's life, and exploring the small church dedicated to her and erected not far away from the medieval ruins, supplies few new ones. It turns out to be a much more modern building than one might think, having been built in the 1930s and erected from demolished cottage walls, on the site of the appositely named Church of Fathoms. Inside swallows are nesting, and they bullet out the door at my arrival, their electric trills alerting the chicks safe in the mud-cup nests to the fact that there's an intruder. I decide not to loiter. It's been chill these past days and insects would have been in short supply. I leave the swallows to it, as they scythe over the fields, gathering brunch for their growing brood.

At St Justinian's I meet David John, the coxswain of the RNLI lifeboats stationed here, whose grandfather was a lifeboat man and his father a coxswain before him. This station has been saving lives since 1869 and they get called out between 40 and 45 times a year. Usually it all turns out well, although David regrets that sometimes his work involves picking up a climber's body, smashed on the rocks, or a body from the sea.

They are planning to move this lifeboat station in two or three years to accommodate a new boat and replace the facilities which are now a century old. It won't go far but it will be an expensive build. As I talk to him on the flight of whitewashed steps that lead down to the station, a boatload of day visitors to nearby Ramsey island disembark. They chatter happy as parakeets. David bids me farewell: he has work to do, and in his case it often is a matter of life or death.

To sum up the colourscape of the pool at Abereiddi you have to run through the gamut of aquamarine, lapis lazuli, ultramarine, and cerulean and still not really manage to sum it up. It's popularly known as the Blue Lagoon, but that's too simplistic, especially as one of the Welsh words for green is *glas*, which also means, a tad confusingly, blue.

Back in 1840 they opened a quarry here on this craggy coast, which produced a stream of broken rock, right up until 1904. The ruins of seven two-roomed cottages from its quarrying heyday make up The Street, which housed sixteen men when the place was busy as a hive and known as Little Brighton. In 1938 there

Traeth Llyfn, Abereiddi

was a huge flood and after that a severe outbreak of typhoid. These events chipped away at the place. After the works closed, fishermen blew a hole, breaching the quarry side and allowing the sea in to create a harbour and thus the blue lagoon.

At the right time of year at Strumble Head you can while away a pleasant hour doing nothing more than watching the harbour porpoises breaking the surface of the waves. For much of the spring and summer there'll be gannets, too, on patrol from their home on Grassholm. These are very striking birds, with their white cigar-shaped bodies and telephone-black wing tips, lifting high in the air before they spot some fish. Then they fold their wings to plunge and the body becomes a living spearhead.

In the distance their island home looks half white and half black, the white being the dense congregation of nesting birds, along with many years deposition of guano, or bird shit. The black is basalt rock, slowly being whitewashed by the 30,000 pairs of birds.

If the southern portion of the Pembrokeshire Coast Path is for casual saunterers, then the northern section is for trainee sherpas – the Ordnance Survey contours tightening in places to something resembling a thick line. But the occasional heart pounding incline is well worth it, not least at Pwll y Wrach, the Witch's Cauldron, a collapsed cave where the edge of the former entrance is left standing as a natural bridge. Stand here and the sound of incoming waves swells as if in a cathedral nave, while a blowhole can spume and spit with rabid energy in the winter.

It's a wild coast, no doubt about that, with cannonades of waves hitting dragon teeth rocks. All the more surprising to find out that the farming couple whose land abuts the Witch's Cauldron once spotted a surfboarder out at sea in the midst of a real hurling tempest. The lifeboat, sent out to help was not best pleased. Surfing in the eye of the storm? Definitely not for me. I'll stick to bar skittles.

Choughs at Wooltack Point, near Marloes

Teifi estuary, Cardigan

Coal mine chimney, near Nolton Haven

Newgale

Gannets at Grassholm

Newport Bay

Druidston Haven, St Bride's Bay

5 Teifi to Dyfi
Seaweed Hair
and Limpet Eyes

Llangrannog

The car park signs near the Co-op in Cardigan warn of the danger of flooding affecting parked vehicles, and today's rain, being a Biblical drenching, makes one pay heed. As I walk alongside the quay, I can barely make out the Teifi Blu Floating Restaurant that might end up atop Ararat if this deluge continues. The few pleasure craft are being hit by an artillery of hail, which fair rattle their timber and plastic hulls.

This scene would have been so different a couple of centuries ago. In the Netpool area of the southern bank of the Teifi, timber would have been stacked high, for this was the epicentre of Ceredigion shipbuilding, with an estimated 1000 people employed here at its peak, with some building hulls and others making the often complicated rigging. In 1816, for instance, there were 323 ships registered here, with a total tonnage of 13,686.

Not far from Cardigan, as the chough flies, stands the iconic Holy Cross church at Mwnt, a simple Christian witness box dating from the 14th century, although there was probably a church here as far back as the Age of Saints, when the likes of Illtud, Teilo, Melangell and Dyfrig spread the good word. Set against the ineffable blue of the flowering sea squill that carpets the humpy hill that rises behind it, the whitewashed walls of the Holy Cross are emphasized, suggesting purity and clarity.

Here in the lee of that 250-foot high hill, redoubtable pilgrims would gather to make the choppy crossing to Bardsey island, across the dangerously changeable seas of Cardigan Bay or otherwise press on to St David's. Stand on the top of the mount, where there was once a preaching cross, and the wind is enough to claim a layer of skin, a veritable flying scourge. One has to admire the strength of conviction of those who would set sail from here in simple craft, in the age before inshore rescue vessels, when faith was the only lifejacket.

Aberporth is a controversial place: unmanned aerial vehicles or drones are launched from the testing base outside the village and given their own airspace when needed. We know about such drones from news headlines, and there have been fears that they've been used to target civilians in the Gaza conflict.

Yet the village itself is peace itself. Overlooking the sandy beach is the benign wooden sculpture of a bottlenose dolphin by Paul Clarke. The seawaters hereabouts are some of the last remaining habitats for these shy, but highly sociable animals, which often live for thirty years and sometimes for fifty. There are about 250 bottlenoses resident in Cardigan Bay and they can be seen pretty much anywhere on the south Ceredigion coast, especially in spring, summer and early autumn. It is a joyous, uplifting spectacle to see them hunting in packs, involving skittering, high speed surface chases, sometimes throwing fish in the air, and often seeming to be doing nothing more than joyously celebrating life in the sea, and the companionship of their fellow cetaceans.

It's a twisting road that snakes down to the cove at Llangrannog, a once bustling fishing harbour where the busyness of netting herring has been replaced by retailing ice cream – and thus a pistachio cone at the Patio comes complete with a fine view of waves. I walk past The Pentre Arms, long famous as a sort of poetic Sorbonne where local bards such as the farmer Dic Jones held spirited lessons and unspun the secrets of *cynghanedd*, that complex Welsh strict metre verse which can be produced with astonishing ease by such masters.

Overhead a female peregrine takes her offspring on a training flight, the youngster yickering excitedly as it tests out its scythe-shaped wings. Standing on the headland on the southern rim of Llangrannog – under a sky of cerulean blue candy flossed with cirrus clouds – I watch auks, pretty much all guillemots, flutter down from ledges to settle on a surface as still as slate.

Miniaturized squadrons of insects reconnoitre the gorse banks whose sulphur-coloured landing beacons guide such tiny visitors towards the nectar.

A raven cronks overhead, this sound an aural hallmark of this stretch of west Wales where these birds with their pick-axe bills and black lozenge-shaped tails are permanent and imposing presences. *Y gigfran*. Which loosely translates as the meat bird, the bird that would first turn up on a battle-field to pick at the slain. While other collective nouns for birds have a ready poetry, such as an exultation of larks, a charm of goldfinches, or a spring of teal, the raven gathers in a dreadful manner, as a murder of ravens. Be wary. Be very wary. Watch out for your ham sandwiches.

Llangrannog is a village whose menfolk have often been in peril on the seas. The church, St Carannog's has plentiful evidence of murderous oceans in the epitaphs on the slate head-stones in its churchyard. David Jones, 34 years old, who died on his way back from Larash, Morocco, and his brother William, who died between Cardiff and Messina. William Lewis, who died at Payta, Peru. James Jenkins, drowned between Swansea and Karrickfergus. The graves bear silent testament to the ghosts of seamen with seaweed hair and limpet eyes. The raging, inconstant sea has claimed master mariners and cabin boys alike, all dragged down to Davy Jones's locker, an unfathomable place where no one can hear you scream, and which some associate with St David, the patron saint both of Wales and of sailors.

Autumn brings the starlings back to Aberystwyth, a glorious end-of-the-pier show as they pixelate the skies, ten thousand of them, which roost here for six months of the year. The collective noun for these gregarious birds is a murmuration and collectively

Bottlenose dolphins off Tresaith

Llangrannog

Llangrannog

Aberystwyth

they do sound like incoming insects, Ceredigion locusts perhaps, out to denude the hills of bracken. Above the rim of Cardigan Bay they wheel and whirl, twist and bank as one, now towards the National Library, then stringing out towards the marina, each individual a swiftly moving feather's width away from the next. Because they seemingly move as one organism, a predator would find it hard to isolate a single bird from the chaotic mass. Scientific studies show that each bird keeps an eye on *exactly* seven other birds, irrespective of their distance, so should a hungry peregrine or other bird of prey decide that a starling is nothing more than a feathery, flying vol-au-vent, this wingtip precision means that they can regroup quickly. Together they make a fine natural history spectacle, an aeronautic display to beat the Red Arrows, even as they start to settle noisily on the pier's ironwork, before chattering into silence.

But although Aberystwyth is all about the safety and warmth of its under-the-pier roost, it is a seaside town with more than its fair share of attractions for humans, too. The old college buildings on the front meld into Marine Terrace with its hotels such as the Queensbridge and Belle Vue, which must need painting every spring after winter's wash of salt spray.

Someone, I think it was the town's youngest ever mayor, Sion Jobbins, once called Aber 'the Athens of west Wales' and there is something to his argument. The National Library, custodian of endless thought and document, has a million maps alone in its collection, and even then you can still get lost in its endless corridors. Then there's the university, claiming levels, like a vineyard, of the same hill at Penglais. And if it is indeed Athens then the equivalent to the port of Piraeus would be Aber harbour, summoned into being by the town's constable in 1280, and since then a place that's seen all manner of trade, from malt drying, through lifeboat construction to anchor making.

Nowadays it's overlooked by those homogenous apartments-with-a-view that have spread like a rash on so many spots along the coast, IKEA-furnished vantage points over the rigging of the pleasure craft which have replaced the herring fleets. It's all so different from the days when Daniel Defoe found a town 'enriched by the coals and lead, which is found in its neighbourhood, and is a populous, but a very dirty, black, smoky place, and we fancied the people looked as if they lived continually in the coal or lead mines.' Those lead mines further up the Ystwyth are long closed but their residues remain. I'll repeat as fact an assertion made some years ago by a local biologist: that there is so much lead in plants such as sea-campion growing on the river's lower reaches, that harvesting the metal would be commercially viable.

The tide is rising, forcing the birds to move: geese abandon their grass cropping and take flight, honking as if they are gulping their own voices. Their greys join those of the sky, and are soon absorbed by them as they fly to safe pasturage. Next some lapwing are dislodged: this tide is moving quickly, claiming the land at a lick. The richly embroidered tapestry of habitats of the Dyfi estuary is Wales's first, and, to date, only UNESCO Biosphere reserve. Part of it lies within the Royal Society for the Protection of Birds' reserve at Ynys-hir and will forever be associated in my mind with William Condry, that doyen of naturalists, who was a staple contributor to the *Guardian*'s Country Diary for over forty years.

Bill and his wife Penny lived at Ynys Edwin, a solid stone house between oak woods and salt marsh, dwelling pretty much as close to nature as it's possible to be. There was a summer when a pair of wild birds nested in their bedroom. Another good example of their oneness with what was around them came one

New Quay

Dunlin at Ynyslas

April, when Bill encountered a male adder, shaking off its winter dormancy. Curious and tender, he stroked the serpent on the head. When I walk the marshes here, he is still with me: he was ever the most quiet companion.

On a winter's day the avian spectacles at Ynys-hir are many and various. Hen harriers quarter the reeds – their long wings outstretched and primary feathers splayed out – alert for pipits and other feathered snacks. Out on the wet grasslands those displaced lapwings butterfly in, their black-and-white plumage engraved against the watery pewter of the sky. Barnacle geese on the river edge bark and yap and Wales's only flock of Greenland white-fronted geese join them, though they are few in number: overall this species continues to dwindle in Wales. Winter thrushes, redwings and fieldfares gorge themselves stupid on a good hawthorn berry harvest, and take high tea among the orange-bright rowan berries on the hillsides overlooking the marsh. They chatter animatedly as they strip the branches, a thrush frenzy, an alfresco berry raid.

Along the Ceredigion coast there are legends of towns under the sea, most famously that of Cantre'r Gwaelod, said to be somewhere in the now drowned environs of Ynyslas or Borth. The story goes that good farmland hereabouts was drained and protected from the sea by strong dykes punctuated by floodgates. One stormy night, in his cups, the keeper of the gate, Seithennyn, neglected to close the gates, thus turning an agricultural area into an Atlantis. The people living here were drowned and all that's left of the place is the occasional pealing of bells, drowned ones, which sound eerie and water-muffled from the weedy depths.

It could happen again, which explains why Alison Heal, the ecologist for Ceredigion Council, has recently been seconded to the £12 million coastal works project at Borth, designed to protect the town against one of those once-in-a-hundred-year storms. For this hard-hat job she's empowered as the ecological clerk of works, overseeing the engineering activity on behalf of bodies such as the Countryside Council for Wales, making sure it doesn't damage the sensitive wildlife habitats hereabouts, say by releasing too much sediment.

It's a massive undertaking, designed to reduce the risks of flooding and erosion in this sometimes storm-battered town for the next 50 years. Over 40,000 tonnes of rock had to be imported from Norway, as they needed many large rocks which were at least six tonnes in weight and a good few that were closer to ten. There were advantages to getting stone from Scandinavia. Moving them by sea saved the equivalent of three thousand return lorry trips.

Alison speaks enthusiastically about some of the marine life special to this stretch of coast, such as *seiri tywod*, or sand masons, little worms that collectively create sandy reefs made up of the myriad casings they throw up as they emerge, only to disappear again.

Alison Heal at Borth

There are other sunken delights in Alison's world. One of the coastal features that mark out this stretch of coast is the fossilized forest, preserved in peat and clay beds. The latter hosts a speciality species, the piddock, a sort of pointy oyster, which is also known as angelwings, as the shell opens as a divine fan after the creature dies. These animals twist themselves down into the clay or sift rock, which is not the most angelic way to go about things.

The Norwegian stones will create an artificial reef that should benefit surfers and wildlife. 'It's already being colonized,' says Alison, listing the 'barnacles, algae and seaweed, the lobsters and crabs, while seals too are showing an interest.'

It's a reminder that under the waves there is ample life and that what we see of the sea is just the surface, with benthic layers overlaying each other, and incredible creatures that live on the bottom and feed on the dandruff of tiny animal parts that eventually settles down to bring them supper. The waves are skin, the sea a great, complicated body.

A new truck arrives carrying more enormous stones to shore up the sea-defences and a giant metal arm drops one to the ground, which quakes, registering somewhere in the lower reaches of the Richter scale. After being courteously ushered behind a safety barrier by a man in a fluorescent jacket, Jerry and I look for a rare bird that's appeared in a wet horse paddock behind the launderette in Borth. It's not there so we have some teacakes in the 'Limit' cafe. The enthusiastic owner shows us a bird book, pointing out a glossy ibis so we can recognize it should it come back. He tells us it nests in the Po valley and somewhere in the Danube. As we saunter outside, Jerry gives me the thumbs up and there it is, not that glossy admittedly under dishwater skies, but its down-curved bill is quite unmistakable as it probes the icy ground. Neither of us visibly twitch, but we do appreciate just how rare it is. In the 19th and 20th century there were only

eleven records of the species in Wales – most of those shot – with the last live one seen in 1910, although a whole flock was blown to Pembrey in Carmarthenshire in 2011. It's certainly declining as a breeding bird in Europe.

The ring on its leg suggests it came from Huelva in Southern Spain. And here it is, under a very wan sun, in the throes of midwinter, feeding behind the Bottle Bank and the community hall. It is insouciantly eating earthworms and grubs to a soundtrack of earthmoving vehicles, a bird both lost and found.

Glossy ibis at Borth

Starlings at Aberystwyth

Aberystwyth pier

Purse-seine net fishermen, Glandyfi

Submerged forest, Ynyslas

6 **Dyfi to Dwyryd**
Stately and
Silvery Progress

Fairbourne

There are few picture windows with such a good picture outside as the Literary Institute in Aberdyfi, with its expansive view of estuary ebb and flow. A raft of duck drifts with the tide. Three cormorants fly upriver in trident formation. Kayakers brave the chill water further along the promenade. Established in 1882, this former bath house and meeting house for the Plymouth Brethren is nowadays a quiet reading room, with a selection of books and the day's paper. It has cases of sea shells, their identifying labels now faded, wiped away by time, and stuffed birds, including a Gyrfalcon alongside commoner birds, from terns to waders. They too are fading fast, all turning into ghost birds in their cage of glass.

Having seen the ibis in the morning, and seen the sea defence work at Borth, both products, one might argue, of climate change, we've arranged to meet a world expert on the subject. Sir John

Houghton co-chaired the Nobel Prize-winning Intergovernmental Panel on Climate Change and lives in a house with even better views of the Dyfi than those from the Literary Institute. He makes a fine Earl Grey and settles us down in a grape arbour in the conservatory to talk.

Born and brought up in the Rhyl area, he developed an interest in nature very early on, and when he was five he was taken up into the clock working of Big Ben and saw and heard the iconic timepiece striking twelve.

There's a clock ticking for some parts of the coast. Having studied such matters how does he see the Welsh coastline changing?

'Some places will be inundated, and some places sunk but it will not be as bad as say, the east of Britain, areas such as East Anglia, and it certainly won't be as desperate as some countries such as Bangladesh, where ten million people who are living under the ten-metre contour will be displaced by rising sea level. Where are they going to go?'

In recent years Wales has seen a great many changes in the natural world, birds changing their nesting patterns and species rare a decade ago, such as little egrets, now nesting here. Perhaps even the morning's ibis was a part of this?

'There are changes affecting species and habitats and there are often profound changes in such things as average rainfall, floods: indeed, extremes of climate are getting far more common. Take the 2003 European heatwave when over 20,000 people died in cities across the continent. There have been heatwaves too in Australia and America. By 2050 such events will be part of any 'normal' year. The same goes for floods, not just from sea level rise but also from increased rainfall.'

Sir John pours some more Earl Grey. Outside the winter sun stroboscopes on the distant sands.

The houses of Fairbourne have been appropriately baptized, as the sea has registered its song, its proximity and its onshore

Sir John Houghton

breezes – Cartref Môr, Cân y Môr, Ger y Môr, Môr Awel, Morlais, Seaward and Stranlea, although there are always eccentric exceptions – Milroo, Karambi and Ilarious, presumably where the local clown lives.

There are few railways in Wales that run for the most part through desert yet the Fairbourne railway is just such a line, as it passes through expanses of sand, cutting through banks of dunes as it scythes through the town: in parts the sandblow has made some of the tracks almost invisible. I'm three months too late to catch the train: it being winter, I can only follow the tracks out towards the mouth of the Mawddach on foot, following the almost Germanically efficient sea defences, past the golf clubhouse and Morfa Ffriog, a marshy stretch where mallards dabble in the shallows. Out toward the mouth of the river the waves are surging and breaking like wild white horses. The gusts mean that one's face is sandblasted, and one's eyeballs scoured by emery paper. It's painful to look directly out to sea.

The earliest railway here was opened in 1895 when the carriages were horse-drawn along a tramway. During the First World War a company called Narrow Gauge Railways Limited

Fairbourne railway

were seeking suitable locations for its 15-inch gauge lines, and in 1916 they purchased the Fairbourne tramway, and a single engine called 'Prince Edward of Wales' was also purchased to provide the locomotive power. Three businessmen from the Midlands purchased the FSR in 1946 and quickly started restoration and, with a mixture of diligence and investment, by 1948 the line was completely re-laid to Barmouth Ferry. This sounds a trifle grander than it actually is. The Harbour View Café doubles up as the Barmouth to Fairbourne ferry station. From here you can take the short hop in a small white boat called *Seren Wen*, aka *Y Chuff*: return fare £2.50. There is no passport control or customs desk when you get to the other side.

On a summer's day the accents in this slate-coloured seaside town are those of Handsworth and Selly Oak, for this is a place with an umbilical to the Midlands, not least the train which rumbles into town over a long wooden bridge.

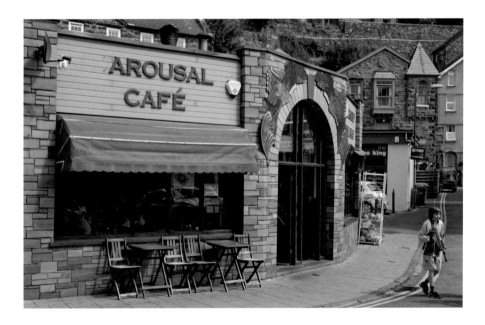

Barmouth

Barmouth, facing Fairbourne, sits on the northern lip of the mouth of the Mawddach, which is unarguably the most beautiful estuary in Wales. The river makes stately and silvery progress, meandering down along a shoulder of Cader Idris. The town had a rich maritime tradition, but after its shipping heyday, it slumped into the doldrums, the wind taken out of its sails quite literally. A decline in exports such as slate, lead, manganese and zinc saw the town in trouble, but it was thrown a lifeline by that railway which reached across the Mawddach estuary via an extraordinary wooden viaduct in 1867. Tall Victorian guesthouses mushroomed on its streets and Queen Victoria's daughter, Beatrice, opened a large church in the town in 1889. Many of the town's houses cling limpet-like to the rock outcrops which form a somewhat stern backdrop to the place.

With its uplifting and prepossessing views, Barmouth had much to admire for the early tourists: it's perhaps little wonder that the first property to be acquired by the National Trust was here. It came courtesy of three Victorian philanthropists who wanted to create 'open air sitting rooms for city dwellers to have a place to breathe.' The particular open-air sitting room they chose was Dinas Oleu, 'Fortress of Light', a hump of rock that dominates the town's skyline, and beyond which is the Panorama Walk with its commanding views of the estuary and the Llawllech mountains beyond. Little wonder Barmouth became a renowned place to stay and walk. It attracted visitors such as the naturalist and evolutionary theorist Charles Darwin and the writer about art and architecture, John Ruskin. As the posters gaily proclaimed this was the place to come 'For Mountains, Sand and Sea.'

My dry stone-walling friend Stuart Fry, who is one of those people who can genuinely wax lyrical for hours about enclosures and hedges and the people who built them, simply loves the walls along the coastal belt between the road and the dunes running between Barmouth and Llanbedr. They are known as 'consumption walls.' which have nothing to do with tuberculosis,

but rather refer to the sheer weight and numbers of stones used to create them, as folk in early medieval times cleared pasture space to plant oats and barley.

Often, individual stones weigh in at nothing less than a couple of tonnes. The walls themselves are the width of a saloon car, and they would have been arranged as walls because 'piles of stone have a habit of finding themselves scattered back around the fields where they came from whereas walls trap them more permanently. Even though they may have no function as boundary markers, they do offer much needed shelter, set as they are at right angles to the prevailing winds.' These are built using an innate sense of physics and knowledge of weather.

West of Llanbedr is Mochras, or Shell Island, created inadvertently by the diversion of the river Artro in 1819 because previously it would have entered the sea to the south. The shore here is one huge cemetery, crunchy underfoot with the calcified remnants of a zillion small sea creatures washed up by storm and high tide.

A diligent expert walking along here could spot two hundred different kinds of shell, especially in winter when oyster shells, scallops, tusks and tellins, whelks and cowries are all washed ashore. Some are tiny, miniature homes for Lilliputian sea creatures, so that twenty separate shells could sit comfortably on the back of a five pence piece. As this stretch of coast hosts one of the biggest campsites in Europe, then presumably a great many shells end up carted away as souvenirs to sit on shelves. But the storms keep bringing them in, some say from Cantre'r Gwaelod, that land buried under the sea to the south. Listen very, very carefully and you may hear those distant bells like marine tintinnabulation, like tuning in to Debussy's Sunken Cathedral. Ringing from the depths. Honest. For those who have ears to listen...

Harlech is one of those coastal towns that congregates around its castle, perched on its crag which features as the great rock of Harlech in the Mabinogi folk tales. With its round corner towers and imposing gatehouse, it stands there solid as an eagle,

Mawddach: the most beautiful estuary in Wales

fronting the sea and protecting a huddle of hotels and houses which have subsequently mushroomed in its lea, mainly on flat land reclaimed from the sea.

Edward I, seized by a great fit of castle building, commanded that it be built between 1283 and 1289, and he employed a highly gifted Savoyard architect, James of St George, to draw up the plans for what would turn out to be a masterpiece of medieval military architecture. But its lofty position and solid defences weren't enough to stop Owain Glyndŵr from seizing it in 1404: it became the epicentre of his marauding activities for five years until he was forced to give it up.

In 1988 Harlech was awash with natural history news when the biggest turtle every recorded was washed up dead. It weighed 916 kg, or just under a tonne and measured three metres, or ten feet nose to tail and it had been entangled in fishing ropes connected to a whelk trap: it transpired that its stomach was full of plastic. The leatherback is the largest of the marine turtles and gets its name from the black, leathery skin that covers its shell. They are unique amongst reptiles in that they have some internal control of their own body temperature, so they can forage in temperatures lower than 5°C and dive to depths of over 1km. The animals, which nest in the Caribbean summer, swim to the coast of the UK to feed on jellyfish, hitching a ride on the currents of the Gulf Stream.

And this isn't the only species which drifts in from such warm waters. In years of jellyfish abundance, when the sea blooms with blue, compass and moon jellyfish, and with wind sailors and barrel jellyfish, basking sharks cruise in towards our coasts, their enormous mouths continually agape as they trawl marine waters. One year the 'jellies' were present in such numbers that they attracted a 1,500-strong super pod of dolphins and their young, an animated marine spectacle that stretched for a mile along the Pembrokeshire coast.

The rare Kemp's Ridley sea turtle, another species normally found in the warm waters of the Gulf of Mexico, was found washed up on the beach at Llanon in Cardiganshire in December 2011, in a year punctuated with a good many sightings of leatherbacks.

The Gulf Stream doesn't just bring in creatures such as turtles and extraordinary species such as sunfish – the world's largest bony fish which can grow up to 3m long and weigh up to 1,360kg or an almighty 3,000lb – it also has a fundamental role in making Wales a place fit to live. The country is on the same line of latitude as Labrador, and were it not for the sea and the balmy beneficence of the Gulf Stream, Wales, as a country, would be well nigh untenable. It's a big global system: the stream consists of a flow of warm water from the southern hemisphere to the north. The Gulf Stream releases heat into the atmosphere in the north Atlantic along northern Europe, and then sinks deep into the ocean flowing back to the south. It warms up the Welsh seas. And land.

Windcheaters were designed for a gusty walk at Traeth Bach, the 'little beach' which forms the southern rim of the twin estuary of the Glaslyn and Dwyryd rivers where it melds with a wild stretch of sandy beach at Morfa Harlech, with its shifting backdrop of dunes held tight by the roots of marram grass. Here the diligent plant seeker will find a poetic and colourful bouquet hidden away: smooth cat's ear and sheep's bit scabious, maiden pink and pyramid orchids; mudwort and moonwort; swarmy bee orchids, balmy heartsease and bladderwort, suitably found in wetter slacks.

On a sunny day you might catch sight of a common lizard, basking between insect hunts, but you'd be lucky indeed to chance upon a sand lizard. Yet Wales's largest population of these jewel-eyed creatures live in these sandy Himalayas – or at least that's what they must look like to an eight-inch-long animal – with half of that length being the tail. Recently reintroduced to the area, they seem to have taken to their windswept Gwynedd home.

Traeth Bach

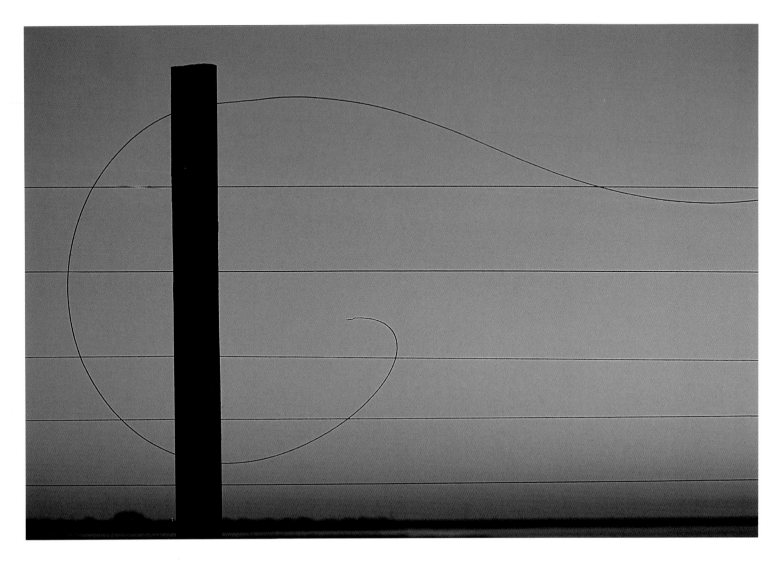

Nearby is a village that once stood on the coast until they moved the coast, took it away, leaving the place stranded. As you pass through Minffordd, a name which means the edge or side of the road, today you'd hardly guess it was once an important coastal community, with a solid trade in woollen goods, wood bark, lime and lead from the hills, and in slate. Small coal would be imported from Pembrokeshire too, not to mention the back-breaking harvesting of mussels and cockles, and fishing, of course. Shipbuilding too was an important employer, and between 1761 and 1821 over fifty vessels were built from scratch at Traeth Mawr, the big beach, including seven sloops, two brigantines, one smack, a wherry and a single cutter. And there was a trade in wine, with imports from Spain and Portugal, and a legion of small hostelries sprang up to sell wine along the coast: indeed two local poets, Rhys Nanmor and Huw Cae Llwyd, travelled to the great pilgrimage centre of Santiago de Compostella on an empty wine ship returning to northern Spain. All this changed when the sea embankment known as the Cob was created in

Barmouth Bridge

nearby Porthmadog, changing the landscape and the ways people passed through it, even though it would take fifty years of reclamation for the treacherous sands to become grasslands.

Before that, travellers who wanted to avoid the long trek around Aberglaslyn would aim for Minffordd, to cross those wild sands at Traeth Mawr, easily the most dangerous part of the route from London to north-west Wales. Between 1770 and 1850, when more than a hundred guides and travel books about Wales were published, many had accounts of the heart-pounding trek across Traeth Mawr, often guided by locals:

> The view of these sands is terrible, as they are hemmed in on
> each side by very high hills, but broken into thousands of irregular
> shapes. At one end is the ocean, at the other the formidable
> mountains of Snowdonia, black and naked rocks which seemed
> to be piled one above the other, the summits of some of them are
> covered with clouds and cannot be ascended. The grandeur
> of the ocean corresponding with that of the mountains, formed
> a majestic and solemn scene…

Some travellers chose to avoid paying guides to take them across the terrible sands: at least seven parsimonious people lost their way and thus their lives. Traeth Mawr was a place to make you quake in your boots, or die in them.

Travellers could stay at some of the coast-side houses as they waited for low tide or more clement weather, and I've been to one of the oldest habitations where even now they keep on finding old coins in the garden, tokens of the trade when Minffordd was a key travel point. Nowadays, as even the car traffic changes courtesy of a new bypass, the village is quieter still. And will become ever quieter, so that standing on the side of the main road you might even hear the far off shush of the sea, the sea which created the village and once upon a time caused it to thrive.

Portmeirion is an astonishing confection, a slightly tongue-in-cheek assemblage of follies, a ragtag assemblage of architectural odds and sods, of cobbled piazzas, campaniles and Florentine domes, which add up to an elegant faux Italian village in North Wales, inspired by such places as Port Grimaud on the Cote d'Azur and made famous by the surreal TV series *The Prisoner*, starring Patrick McGoohan and Virginia Maskell.

Stroll around this eccentric architecture and you can spot all manner of styles, from sham to substantial with Jacobean, Gothic, Bavarian vernacular and Regency all part of the dizzy mix. It was put together much in the way that Harold Steptoe decorated his home in the BBC scrapyard comedy *Steptoe and Son*. Clough Williams-Ellis magpied his way through an assortment of fallen buildings, collecting bits of masonry, or sometimes much larger features and carting them back to his evolving village. The colonnade overlooking the village green was once owned by

Fairbourne

TOLLS TO BE TAKEN AT THIS GATE.

For every Horse or other Beast of Draught drawing any Coach, Sociable, Berlin, Landau, Chariot, Vis-a-vis, Chaise, Calash, Chaise-marine, Curricle, Chair, Gig, Whisky, Caravan, Hearse, Litter, Waggon, Wain, Cart, Dray, or other Carriage, any Sum not exceeding One Shilling:

For every Horse, Mare, Gelding, or Ass, laden or unladen, and not drawing, the Sum of Sixpence: but if there shall be more than one such Horse, Mare, Gelding, Mule, or Ass, belonging to the same Person, then the Sum of Sixpence shall be paid for one of them only, and the Sum of Three-pence only for every other of them:

For every Drove of Oxen, Cows, or Neat Cattle, any Sum not exceeding Five Shillings per Score, and so in proportion for any greater or less Number:

For every Drove of Calves, Pigs, Sheep or Lambs, any Sum not exceeding Three Shillings and Sixpence per Score, and so in proportion for any greater or less Number:

And for every Person crossing or passing on Foot, without any Beast or Carriage, any Sum not exceeding Two-pence.

Toll charges, Minffordd

a Quaker copper smelter in Bristol. The Town Hall, or Hercules Hall, in Portmeirion is what Williams-Ellis described as a 'fallen building,' namely rescued parts from the sale of Emrall Hall from Flintshire. Clough bought the ceiling and doors and later added a cupola made out of an old pig boiler. The shield of arms over the doors is the Red Hand of Ulster. Ingrid Bergman danced here when she was filming *The Inn of Sixth Happiness* nearby. The more time you spend here, decoding the buildings, appreciating the way it all dovetails together, the more you delight at the way it's all come together, this zany, marvellous vision.

Clough Williams-Ellis, the man who also mapped out the Snowdonia National Park amongst other things, had a dream of creating 'a holiday retreat for the discerning' when he bought the Aber Ia peninsula from his uncle. The name, which translates as Ice Mouth, had too chill a ring for Clough, so he devised his own portmanteau name, with reference to the port which used to take slate from here and Meirion being a reference to the ancient local administrative unit, or hundred. It also had echoes of one of his favourite Italian places, Portofino.

Standing on a bluff overlooking the widening river Dwyryd, which drains the Vale of Maentwrog as it opens out onto the sandy expanse of Traeth Bach, somehow its location couldn't be more conducive to building a fantasy. It surveys the low, island hump of Ynys Gifftan and, beyond that, the steep slopes of Moel y Geifr and the Rhinogydd, which rise in harmony with the great ancient massif of Ardudwy, or the Harlech Dome, across the water. Hilaire Belloc loved this coast of the Irish Sea:

> There is no corner of Europe that I know, not even the splendid
> amphitheatre standing in tiers of High Alpine Wall around Udine,
> which moves me with the awe and majesty of great things
> as does this mass of the northern Welsh mountains seen from
> this corner of their silent sea.

A view of Snowdon from the Cob

Harlech beach

Portmeirion

7 Dwyryd to Abermenai

Garbled Songs
in the Rigging

Near Aberdaron

A view of Pen Llŷn from Moel-y-gest, Porthmadog

e are about to leave Eifionydd, the name given to this commote (an old unit of land and population, still commonly used today). But we have time enough to pause to look at the skyline of Criccieth which is dominated by its castle, perched imposingly on a rocky tor.

Many schoolchildren will have read and enjoyed Robert Graves's poem called 'Welsh Incident' which starts mid-story…

'But that was nothing to what things came out
From the sea-caves of Criccieth yonder.'
What were they? Mermaids? dragons? ghosts?'
Nothing at all of any things like that.'
What were they, then?' 'All sorts of queer things…

He might have been inspired by the smooth, hunchbacked rocks that you can see when the tide's out as you walk toward Llanystumdwy, once home to Welsh wizard politician David Lloyd George and nowadays to travel writer Jan Morris. Look over your shoulder as you head for the mouth of the Dwyfor – see, one of the monsters has moved, it may be following you.

Llŷn is a peninsula wreathed in legend, the wind carrying the wails of the drowned onto a jagged coastland, the myths settling as pockets of mist in mushroomed field hollows. On the map it reaches out a Pre-Cambrian rocky arm into the sea, trying to seize the apple that is Bardsey island, always tantalisingly just out of reach. The mainland is a landscape studded with tiny white cottages and ancient field patterns, and Llŷn is a heartland of the Welsh language, even though it's a heart more sclerotic than it once was. Its name has the same root as the Irish Leinster, and there are plentiful names derived from the Irish on the maps. Gwyddel. Trwyn y Gwyddel. Neigwl.

It also has its pleasure palaces. The man who transformed

the post-war British holiday, Sir Billy Butlin, opened a camp at Pen-y-Chain near Pwllheli in 1947, having taken over the naval training camp known as HMS *Glendower*. For the next fifty years redcoats and nightly variety shows brought flocks of funseekers to enjoy the slightly regimented chalet life and relentless fun. It's now the Hafan y Môr Holiday Park, and Sir Billy, with his outsize cigars and habit of visiting his camps unannounced, is relegated to a small but vibrant chapter in British Social History, summed up in three words 'Hi De Hi.'

Pwllheli is the great metropolis of Llŷn, with its population of almost 4,000. Its general topography very much changed when they built the marina, Yr Hafan, here. A report in 2002 suggested the marina brought with it 200 jobs and injected £200 million into the local economy, but the chill winds that have been blowing these past few years have affected Pwllheli marina as much as elsewhere. Where there used to be a waiting list for berths now

Caravan park, Pwllheli

there are many empty spaces, although the marina's owners, Gwynedd County Council, have undertaken to improve matters, dredging the approach waters and freezing berthing fees. When it was built, and later as proposals were mooted for its expansion from 420 to 700 berths, the marina sparked real controversy over its potential effects on the Welsh language. This was the town, after all, that saw the first-ever weekly Welsh language newspaper, *Utgorn Rhyddid* or the Trumpet of Freedom, and in 1925 Plaid Cymru, the Party of Wales, was formed at a public meeting in the town. The language can be heard pretty much anytime on Y Maes, the commercial crossroads at the heart of the town. Ancient and steely, its tenacity is being sorely tested nowadays as waves of new settlers choose such places to retire.

Not very far in truth from Pwllheli's gin and tonics and jolly weekend sailors, St Hywyn's church, almost on the shore at Aberdaron is a world removed. It offers shelter for the soul.

> Break, break, break
> On thy cold stones O Sea!

The Tennyson lines seem appropriate as one wave-watches from the beach at Aberdaron, in the shadow of the church. Out there, a relentlessness of waves rhythms in. If we measure out our lives in heartbeats, then the waves measure out time on a much grander scale.

It's as good a place as any around the Welsh coast to ponder the language of waves, from swell waves to constructive waves, riptides to backwash. Waves are formed, of course, when wind blows across the surface of the sea, and the ones in front of me started life a long way away. The longer the wind blows, the bigger the waves, and the steepness and rake of a beach will affect their size and shape as well. And there are three principal types – surging waves that never actually break; spilling waves

which appear when the top of the wave tumbles down the front of a wave, and dumping waves that break with great force in shallow water. These can be a dangerous variety, normally at low tide when the sand banks are shallow and there is less water into which the waves can break.

By way of defying the sea and its energies my daughters and I play tic-tac-toe, skimming some smooth pebbles across the surface of the waves, using the very pebbles they have pushed onshore and smoothed to a gloss. One small pebble, the size of one's palm skips eleven, then twelve times before dropping without a sound. It'll be back.

Here at Aberdaron one of the most important aspects of wave action to ponder is refraction, whereby waves in shallow water are retarded more than those in deep water, so that the waves' crests become curved. This shapes headlands, concentrating wave energy around them while in bays the energy is diffused, spread out, resulting in the cliffs of headlands and the beaches of bays such as Aberdaron Bay. Shaped by millennia of waves of all three types, it curves out toward the headland at Trwyn y Penrhyn and beyond that the two gull islands, Ynys Gwylan Fawr and Ynys Gwylan Fach. In the other direction it has created Pen y Cil and a small stretch of coast punctuated by no fewer than five small landing coves, safe havens in succession, at Porth Simdde, Porth Meudwy, Porth Cloch, Porth y Pistyll and Hen Borth.

All that wave pondering is thirsty work so we retire to the log fire at the Ship, run by Alun Harrison and his very extended family. Luckily it includes his 44-year-old brother Steven, who fishes around here for crab and lobster, which means we can try the homemade crab bhajis washed down with Cardigan Bay bitter.

Morning sees cascades of light, a day of startling visual epiphany. Light bolts hit the land like celestial searchlights. A day for climbing up above Aberdaron, to gain proper vantage over this brilliant display. It won't last long.

Porth Ysgo

In a sense every single stretch of coast is land's end. But when you get to the National Trust-owned Braich y Pwll at Uwchmynydd on Mynydd Mawr, you get the pronounced sense that this chough-haunted finisterre really is where the land is swallowed up up by the sea, especially as you look out toward Bardsey island, or Ynys Enlli, which translates as the isle of swirling currents. It's a final morsel in the grand scheme of things, the scheme wherein oceans engulf and land retreats, where time means attrition and geology decay.

Just to the south of this headland at Porth Felen in 1974 a deep sea diver chanced upon a special find, namely an ancient anchor which came from a Mediterranean merchant ship from the first or second century BC, evidence that such traders came this far north.

The stretch of water between the mainland and Bardsey is nowadays called Y Swnt, or Sound, which can be a treacherous stretch of racing water, but it was once upon a time called Ffrydiau Caswennan because Gwennan, or Gwenonwy, King Arthur's sister, lost her life in its swirling waters when her ship sank. A rock

Y Swnt and Bardsey Island

called Maen Gwenonwy just out to the sea east of Aberdaron, gives tantalizing etymological back-up to this Arthurian connection, as does the fact that Llŷn people refer to star clusters such as Ursa Major, Orion and Lyra as Arad Arthur, Hudlath Arthur and Telyn Arthur, respectively Arthur's plough, wand and harp. All helping to shore up some people's belief that Bardsey was the mythical Avalon.

To properly appreciate the island, you have to go there. The brontosaurus hump of Bardsey in the distance starts to assume detail, to gain form and line as the boat cuts across the pumped waters of the sound towards the safe haven of Y Cafn, passing Trwyn y Fynwent or Graveyard Head, Traeth Ffynnon being Well Beach and Pen Cristin. The square-cut red-and-white lighthouse, built in 1821, seems redundant by day, other than when a San Franciscan style mist rolls in, and the foghorn sends out its almost sub-sonic warning boom. Then the lolling grey seals on the rocks ululate like muezzin, or keeners, mourning lost sailors.

The boat, burning diesel, chops against the waves. Overhead, an arctic skua, a pirate of Northern skies, tries to force a tern to drop the fish in its bill. On we go. Bobbing markers show where the lobster pots lie. They're rich waters around here. Indeed William Bingley, recounting his excursions around North Wales in 1800, noted that the 'collecting of lobsters and crabs occupied most of the time of the inhabitants of Bardsey Island.'

Once on land, visitors are often taken aback by the number of houses on this remote rock, with some of the farmhouses being more than substantial. Tŷ Capel. Nant. Hendy. Cristin. Tŷ Newydd, Tŷ Nesaf. Tŷ Bach. Carreg Bach. Plas Bach. Carreg. Tŷ Pellaf. Rhedynogoch. There was once a substantial community on this isle, with, even in modern times, its own King. It's also home to *afal Enlli*, a unique type of apple, that can fruit even in the eye of the storm. And Afallon is the Welsh for Avalon. Odd, that.

It's an old saw that twenty thousand saints are buried on Bardsey and that three trips to Ynys Enlli was considered equivalent to one to Rome. In the so-called Age of Saints it was a focal point for the early Christian church: reputedly St Cadfan started to build a monastery here in the sixth century. There's no doubt that it's a sacred place, not just because of the apparatus of religion, from the chapel to the remains of the old monastery. It's in the rocks, and the sad hymns of the seals, and the tiny percussive popping of gorse pods.

The coast curving eastwards away from Bardsey and Aberdaron is punctuated by many more little coves and mini-harbours such as Porth Llanllawen, Porth Iago, Porth Ferin, Porth Ysgaden, Porth Oer and Port Widlin. Porthdinllaen is postcard picturesque, with its fish crates and trailers, its lifeboat station and offshore beacon at Carreg y Chwislen, and the white snaggle-toothed strand of old cottages known as Hen Borth looking out at Pen Cim and Penrhyn Nefyn. It also has the tideline pub, Tŷ Coch, with its name spelled out on the roof, presumably to attract passing paragliders to drop in to slake their thirsts, not to mention the more pedestrian explanation of attracting walkers coming in over the golf course above. One of the pub's former landladies, Jane Ellen Jones, doubled up as harbour master, a redoubtable lady in a time when people were more generally tough, and when this was just one port among many on Llŷn: during a survey in 1524 a total of eighteen ports were listed where ships could land.

Porthdinllaen is another of those places where you can sense the ghost of a long-gone industry, when kilns baked lime and fish were cured in harbourside sheds. But most of all they're the spectres of shipbuilders and their creations, the work of callous-palmed men such as James Owen, Evan Ellis and Hugh Hughes. Flat bottomed schooners or sloops, designed to deal with shallow landings and hard rocks, were built on the beach, maybe 50 of them over the years, while, onshore, skilled men such as David Rice Hughes sewed and shaped the sails for these hardy craft.

It's hard also to visualize the mercantile comings and goings, the busy sea trade which took bricks, salt, barley and bricks to Swansea and brought in culm from Llanelli and limestone from Cork. Think of the *Speedwell*, returning here in 1624 loaded with its great variety of cargo, with linen, tobacco pipes, ferrous sulphate, hops, pepper and American logwood for dyeing cloth. Other ships at the time were weighted down with anything from wooden heels to fire grates, treacle to vinegar.

In 1844 some more Parliamentary votes in its favour might have seen Porthdinllaen developed instead of Holyhead as the principal Welsh link with Ireland. But it was not to be, and just as shipbuilding dwindled so too did its ambition as a port grow crabbed. Nowadays Porthdinllaen trades in the expectations and satisfactions of tourists.

Nefyn, too, has had a long connection with the sea. As far back as 1293 the village had two ships registered with a value of twenty shillings as well as 68 fishing nets worth two shillings, and this at a time when an ox was worth five shillings. A hundred years later there was evidence of trade between France and Llŷn. By the mid 18th century there were claims that no fewer than five thousand barrels of salted herring were exported from Nefyn. But the sea is fickle and some years harvests were very poor, while in glut years so many fish were netted that the overstock had to be ploughed into the fields as manure. Luckily the average catch in Nefyn was high: arguments made in favour of creating a turnpike road between London and Llŷn were built around the need simply to facilitate the passage to market of Nefyn herring.

And there can still be spectacular days of herring fishing. Ask Dafydd Phillips, a twinkle-eyed, 57-year-old fisherman who's been working the inshore waters hereabouts since pretty much the time he learned to walk. One night about five years ago, he set three nets. Returning in the morning in his small boat he ironically calls '*Y Tanc*' or 'The Tank', he found they had caught no fewer than 12,000 herring. Every single person he knew ate herring that day. And the next. And the day after. Some grew tiny silvery scales on the backs of their hands.

The sea's in Dafydd's blood, certainly on his mother's side, with a lineage of schooner captains and seadogs going back to 1732. Not that he's been out too much on the sea of late. The wintry gales have put paid to that. 'Any wind that's got a west or a north west about it, well forget it.' On such days he's often found smoking a fag in one of the tatterdemalion fisherman's huts on the seaward rim of the beach.

While the other huts have cutesy Welsh names such as Hafod, Tynlon, Bron Y De and Bryn Coch, the signs on his door give some clues to his slightly mischievous character: one proclaims 'Piss Off I'm Busy' while the other announces 'Ship's Bar Open: 0900-0859.' Here he'll show you the nets he makes himself, or show off the trophies he's won with his son Matthew, a head chef in Criccieth. Each year there's a mackerel race to raise money for the RNLI. The winner is simply the person who catches the most mackerel over a two-hour period. One fine August day, using bait no more sophisticated than rods and strings of six white feathers and hooks they caught a silvery total of 1,900 of the zebra-striped fish. In a hundred and twenty minutes.

Even though there are occasional red letter days, when the sea seems beneficent and superabundant with fish, Dafydd bemoans the fact that in the half-century since he first fished Nefyn as a nipper, stocks have been declining, which he suggests may be to do with overfishing. 'It's like the Dead Sea here sometimes. That's what we call it. The dead sea.' His eyes dim slightly as he makes his point.

Salt was necessary for the trade in fish, with much of it coming from Ireland and subject to a punishing rate of tax, twelve times what the actual producer was paid, which led to a spate of salt smuggling. This suited some Llŷn people for a certain maritime lawlessness has ever prevailed around its coasts, with pirates such as Sir John Wyn ap Huw of Bodfel using Bardsey as a headquarters for plundering and attendant storage of booty.

North-east of Nefyn the coast is all Gothic overhang and guillemot colonies at Trwyn y Gorlech and Trwyn y Tâl, where Yr Eifl plunges into the sea as an episode of landscape high drama, with sheer drops of rock protecting small communities such as Porth y Nant and Nant Gwrtheyrn, now home to the National Language Centre.

It's well worth oxygenating the blood and toning up the calf muscles by climbing some of the loftier slopes of Yr Eifl to reach Tre'r Ceiri, one of the best preserved and once most densely populated Iron Age hill forts in Britain. You can see the remains of some 150 houses and in places walk through a door which still has its lintel intact, connecting one with someone who'd walked through the self-same place a long, long time ago. There are terraces and enclosures for crops and animals, and a real sense of commanding the view, which includes the lizard's spine of ancient rocks reaching out towards the westernmost points of Llŷn, where the setting sun pinks the rocks as it slowly sinks into the sea.

Some of the hills on Llŷn have been worked very hard by man, nowhere more so perhaps than the extensive granite quarry on Garn Fôr above Trefor, which is hollowed out like a rotten tooth to the extent that it is most commonly known as Mynydd y Gwaith, Work Mountain.

Dinas Dinlle is fortuitously protected by a defiant sea-wall, even though the waves today hurl themselves towards the shore as if they are hungry to eat the Taste of India restaurant, the gift shops and the children's play area. A cappuccino froth of foam builds up on the pebbly shore, as the sea grows rabid, making an ever madder land grab. But there is one name among the businesses in this seashore stretch of a village which spells this place out as special, a place of legend, namely Bwyty Lleu.

The name Dinas Dinlle derives from '*Din*' meaning fort and '*lle*' derived from Lleu. According to the vivid folk tale, the Fourth Branch of the Mabinogi, it was here that the warrior and magician Lleu Llaw Gyffes was brought up. The boy aimed a needle at a bird's leg and broke it. Arianrhod commented that 'the fair boy has a deft hand', which provides his name.

And as if to confirm the links between Dinas Dinlle and a past more mythical than mystical, offshore, seen in glimpses among the surge, is a single rock called Caer Arianrhod. One day Math follows Gwydion to Arianrhod's castle where he tells her that the boy is her son. She refuses to acknowledge or name the boy. The following day Gwydion conjures a ship out of seaweed and leather and he and the boy sail to Caer Arianrhod near Dinas Dinlle...

Stand here long enough and you might see it hove into view, as substantial as dream, the wind singing garbled songs in the rigging.

Dafydd Phillips, Nefyn fisherman

Porth y Nant

Penrhyn Glas, near Llithfaen

Tre'r Ceiri

Grey Seals, Bardsey Island

8 **Anglesey**

The Giantess's Apron

Llŷn from Newborough

That Welsh national treasure, the historian John Davies, once suggested that the two greatest British contributions to the world were Ordnance Survey maps and bitter beer. So I try both, perusing the Landranger 114 for Anglesey with its statue of the Marquess of Anglesey on the cover, and a glass of sublime Felinfoel beer to hand. Clockwise round the island seems best, and the area in the south west, at seven o' clock, seems like a good place, or time to start.

As you begin to leave the mainly Corsican pine plantations of Newborough Forest to walk towards Llanddwyn Island, the sea vistas become expansive and dramatic, with the peaks of Snowdonia competing with the spiny sweep of Llŷn for your attention. A sandwich tern skirricks as it patrols the surf for fish glimmer. There is an ozone tang of seawater mixed with the bracing iodine aroma of drying seaweed. Rock pipits zippily pick insects from the air above glistening pebbles. The sun is a brilliant pearl.

It's not a long walk but it does take you into another realm. On a balmy day the views over to Dinas Dinlle are transcendent. The triadic peaks of Yr Eifl puncture the sky over Llŷn, while Garn Fadryn is a far prospect, seemingly sloping into the waves. Nearer to you is the little islet of Ynys y Cranc, or crab island, and another named after a bellringer, Ynys y Clochydd with, nearby Porth y Clochydd, where the aforementioned bellringer, or sexton presumably, anchored his boat.

Llanddwyn isn't really an island as it takes a really high tide to cut it off from the mainland, yet it's an evocative if small nose of land, with the white, windmill-like lighthouse on the tip guiding sailors away from danger.

Geologically speaking you have to walk through and over stands of pillow lava to get to the island's more solid rocks. These pillows were formed by undersea volcanic eruptions, evidence of the great forces once at work on this land-and-sea scape, tossing it into being as earth met both fire and water, quenching the ocean's thirst and extinguishing land's fire at one and the same time.

Romantically speaking it's a place connected with Santes Dwynwen, the patron saint of lovers, or the Welsh equivalent to St Valentine. Legend has it she was one of no fewer than two dozen daughters of Brychan Brycheiniog, the prince of Brecon. She fell in love with a man called Maelon but spurned his advances, choosing instead to pray for a potion which could release her from the chains of this unhappy love. Sadly, on drinking it, the young man turned to ice. To break this spell Dwynwen prayed for three things: the revival of Maelon, the happiness of all lovers, and that she should never herself be married, choosing rather to retreat to the solitude of the island. In turn it became a veritable magnet for pilgrims, so many in fact during the Tudor age that they were able to build a substantial 16th-century chapel, now in ruins. It's one of a small assortment of buildings on the island, from that windmill-inspired lighthouse to the row of pilots' cottages, built by the Caernarfon Harbour Trust in the early 19th century, all adding further interest to this enchanting, elegant finger of rock.

The village of Malltraeth is, for many, synonymous with the artist Charles Tunnicliffe, who sat for many a patient hour at Malltraeth Pool, where wading birds and wildfowl have grown used to people, and would certainly pay little heed to a quiet man such as he with his sketchbook and pencil, keen to register wild wonder as directly as possible. Tunnicliffe spent thirty years living in a house called Shorelands at Malltraeth and his work is sublime in both detail and spirit. Flights of wigeon bank onto the page. His pencil work magicked godwits to needle soft mud. Lines of dunlin wheeled left to right in tight formation. All captured by this quiet Cheshire man who clearly loved his adoptive island, even as he patiently captured its seasons and its discreet colours.

There are churches, and there are churches in the sea and St Cwyfan's is one of the latter. When she's alone here, especially in the winter, the vicar of St Cwyfan's Church-in-Sea Madalaine Brady feels that 'the boundary between heaven and earth is thin.' With the door open 'being here by oneself is a very fulfilling thing,' she maintains.

Madeleine, who moved to North Wales thirty years ago and has been in the parish of Llanfeilog these past fifteen, loves the sense of age in this stranded church, along with the sheer simplicity of the place, the feeling that 'it takes away all the trappings.' One of the first women priests to be ordained, the Rev. Brady used to visit the church during school holidays from her Lancashire home, little suspecting that one day her duties as Rural Dean in south-west Anglesey would include care for this ancient, sea-bound church. She holds three services here each year, all in the summer months and each dependent on a low tide, knowing that it's 'special for many people, because of its great age.'

The church stands on an island called Cribinau, near the village of Aberffraw. Old maps show the church standing on the mainland of Anglesey but erosion by the sea of the boulder-clay cliffs has since separated the church from the mainland. In complete ruin by the 19th century, money was then raised to create the huge sea defence walls which give the church its distinctive shape.

Founded in the seventh century the present building probably dates back to the 12th or 13th century. It's a place where the sermons are accompanied by the sussuration of the sea, lapping and licking the rocks outside, where seabirds can be a raucous congregation competing with the hymns sung by the dedicated congregation inside.

If you're interested in Neolithic recipes, I know just the place to go. A couple of miles north-west of Aberffraw, at the highest point of the Mynydd Cnwc headland overlooking Trecastle Bay

The Reverend Madalaine Brady, Vicar of St Cwyfan's

stands a chambered burial tomb known as Barclodiad y Gawres, or the Giantess's Apron. It looks more intact than it actually is, as the site was renovated in the early 1950s and now sports a modern glass-topped mound. Here excavations have unearthed evidence of the preparation of a strange, inexplicable ritual stew with fishy, possibly magical ingredients such as wrasse, eel, and whiting, not to mention frog, toad, grass snake and a handful of small rodents. On encountering such a weird *lobsgows* – as they call soup, or *cawl* in North Wales – it is very hard not to think of the three witches in Shakespeare's *Macbeth* and their cackling 'hubble' and 'bubble', as they added 'fillet of fenny snake', 'toe of frog' and 'lizard leg' to their cauldron with its basic stock made of toad juice.

To add to the mystery of the 'Apron', excavators also found a fine series of carved stones. The meaning of the pecked geometric patterns is now lost to us. Maybe they meant 'Season with salt and pepper to taste.'

No dawdling. Too much concertinaed into this small isle, so much so that at South Stack you can actually see the rocks folding, pressured into arches by earth forces beyond imagination.

On a May day, or any day of spring blessedness, small galaxies of flowers sparkle in the maritime heathland: thrift illumines pink, florets of sea campion coruscate small trails of white light, bird's-foot trefoil burns carmine yellow, and kidney vetch sets off tiny purple fireworks of vivid petals. One species, the marvellously named spatulate fleawort is found here at South Stack and here only. It's not really much to look at, a sort of ragwort of the rocks, but unique is unique.

South Stack is also one of the most dependable places in Wales to see chough, with some nine pairs nesting here, or two per cent of the entire UK population. This lovely crow with its scarlet, down-curved bill and matching legs likes probing among the tough grasses of cliff tops. In the air the black feathers splay as it turns into the wind, its call the very essence of such wild places.

Holyhead

Holyhead is nowadays synonymous with Stena Seaways, port of departure for ferries and catamarans, and an international place for a very long time. But Holyhead has history. It was the western edge of the Roman Empire. The first Irish packet station was set up here to carry mail to armies stationed in Ireland. In the 18th century a trip from Ireland could last well over 24 hours. The first yacht seen in British waters was wrecked offshore. A Confederate arms buyer once met an agent from the South in Holyhead to acquire hundreds of rifles and revolvers. It has plenty of history.

In the boom years of copper production on Anglesey the village of Amlwch grew at a dizzying rate, far outpacing the growth of Cardiff, say. The huge ore deposits of nearby Parys Mountain, systematically exploited by the 'Copper King' Thomas Williams, touchstoned a hundred years of building and expansion. At its peak it had five times the population of Cardiff.

The village of Moelfre, halfway along the eastern side of Anglesey, is famous for its lifeboat station. It's a treacherous stretch of coast, with sixty vessels wrecked here just between 1825 and 1827. One of the worst, and thus most famous, wrecks was that of *Royal Charter*, ironically on the last leg of a voyage from Australia to Liverpool when a force 12 hurricane threw her onto rocks near Moelfre in October 1859 with the loss of some 450 people. The fact that she was carrying a huge amount of gold bullion spawned many tales of locals getting rick quick, even though the majority of the precious metal, a third of a million pounds' worth, was recovered. It was enough of an event to attract that supreme teller of tales, Charles Dickens, to visit the scene and he paid tribute to the local rector, the Reverend Hughes from Llanallgo, who wrote over a thousand letters of condolence.

Penmon was once home to the cell of St Seiriol. He might have had a solid reputation as a holy man but that was as nothing to his reputed prowess as a road builder. Apparently he had another hermitage across the water at Penmaenmawr, and to facilitate travel between the two, had a rock pathway built across the mouth of the Menai Strait. According to *Hanes Helig ap Glanawg* 'Sythence this great and lamentable inundation of Cantre'r Gwaelod, being the kingdom of Helig, the way and passage being stopped in this strait in regard the sea was come in and did beat upon the rock at Penmaenmawr, this holy man Seiriol, like a good hermit did cause a way to be broken and cut through the main rock, which is the only passage that is to pass through that strait.'

Puffin Island, a chip off the old limestone block of south eastern Anglesey, and therefore contiguous with the Great Orme to the east, has had many names over the centuries: it has been Priestholm, Ynys Seiriol and, according to Wales's first travel

Settling pools at Parys Mountain

Eglwys-yn-y-môr, the Church of Sant Cwyfan, near Aberffraw

Porth Wen, near Amlwch

writer, Giraldus Cambrensis, it has also been known as Ynys Lenach. When he visited he found it 'inhabited by hermits, living by manual labour, and serving God. It is remarkable that when, by the influence of human passions, any discord arises among them, all their provisions are devoured and infected by a species of small mice, with which the island abounds, but when the discord ceases, they are no longer molested.' Were life an Enid Blyton novel this small rock, now home to gulls and plants such as alexanders, burdock, hemlock and henbane, might be called 'The Island of the Invisible Puffins,' and this would be close to the truth of it.

Thomas Pennant, however, in his *Tours in Wales* noted puffins that 'incessantly squall round, alight and disappear into their burrows; or come out, stand erect, gaze at you in a most grotesque manner, then take flight. Some few save themselves the trouble of forming holes and will dispossess the rabbits who, during the puffin season, retire to the other side of the island.' Even later travellers, such as the author of the *Cambrian Traveller's Guide* of 1840 noted they were there in 'immense number.' But seeing a puffin here would nowadays be cause of celebration. When rats, presumably from a wrecked ship, made landfall on the island, the population of these comical little auks dwindled, eventually to nothing, although some naturalists suggest that the disappearance of the puffins might have been down to other factors.

If only the puffins knew... In a grey building set within the old quarry at Penmon there are no fewer than two million fish, swimming in the tanks of a state-of-the-art fish farm established in 2002, which produces 1000 tonnes of sea bass each year. The Greek company that ran it found itself in difficulties at the end of 2011 and there were fears for the thirty or so workers, not to mention all those fish, but a buyer was eventually found.

The puffins, meanwhile, dream of wire cutters and that shimmering nirvana of sea bass. There must be a way in...

Arctic terns at the Skerries

South Stack

Near Rhoscolyn

Penmon and Puffin Island

Wylfa

9 Abermenai to Conwy
The Hearts of the Troublesome Welsh

Menai Bridge

The coast is flat and wet north of Dinas Dinlle and Morfa Dinlle is most defnitely lapwing country as the road turns towards Fort Belan, notable for being the only purpose-built fortress of the American Revolution on this side of the Atlantic Ocean.

At the time of the Napoleonic wars in the late 18th century, life was turbulent and in Wales there was the threat of coastal invasion by the French. This was also a time of hostility between America and the U.K. It is strange for us today to imagine unfriendly American ships in our waters, but the reality of the threat became obvious when privateers operating at sea captured several of our ships, notably two post office ships which operated between Holyhead and Dublin.

Thomas Wynn, who at the time was Constable of Caernarfon, was aware of the threat and decided to make a bold military decision to build a fort on the tip of the Dinlle Peninsula. He realized both the vulnerability and strategic importance of this point as it overlooks the narrow entrance to the Menai Strait which runs between the mainland and the isle of Anglesey. It is the marine access point to the North Wales coast and the city of Liverpool which even then was a port of international importance.

Initially the fort was garrisoned by Wynn's own troops and his actions and loyalty were rewarded with a peerage. The fort then became part of the chain of defences against the threat of French invasion. It also guards the entrance to Y Foryd, a tidal bay which at high tide looks like an inland sea, and, in winter is a veritable wonderland of waterfowl, a cavalcade of birds. The first to notice one's arrival are the redshank, sentinels of the marshes, setting off alarm calls very much as blackbirds do on dry land. Out on the water wigeon whee-o, flocks of hundreds of them waiting for the water to recede so they can continue grazing the tough grasses. A pair of snipe zig-zag away, their long

bills looking like kebab sticks. And then, as the footpath ends just opposite Warren Farm, two parties of brent geese hove into view. Up close, these small, dark geese are ineffably beautiful – black heads, charcoal plumage, shadow patterns of their plumage reflected in the still water.

The northern banks of the North Wales mainland and the southern rim of Anglesey are separated from the mainland by the fifteen-mile-long Menai Strait. The strait was carved out of an existing valley by the effects of ice, meltwater and glaciation during the recent Ice Ages, assuming its present shape about 5000 BC, several thousand years after the Ice Age that created Anglesey itself in the wake of huge and sustained sea floods.

The Strait forms a geological border just as much as a watery, salty one: on the northern side, the rocks of Anglesey are Pre-cambrian, while the mainland is largely Cambrian and Ordovician. Much of the water is bordered by steep wooded banks, with sand and mud flats at either end. It is a various and variegated coast, with much to see. The Strait is fished and sailed on, its watery treasurelands have been much photographed and documented. Sailors, fair weather and experienced, use its waters for relaxation and exhilaration because the Strait is subject to fierce tidal currents. These can reach up to 8 knots (or 15 km/h) in particularly in the narrow region between the two bridges – Thomas Telford's suspension bridge at Menai Bridge, crossing the rapid currents of the Swellies, and Robert Stephenson's Britannia Bridge.

The direction of water flow changes during the course of the day, due to the differing times of highest and lowest tides at either end. This leads to the common (but untrue) folk legend that the same water remains in the Strait, simply being shuttled back and forth. The sheltered waters of the Menai Strait provide excellent conditions for growth of marine algae, which achieve unusually large sizes in these waters. Rocky areas shelter

Foryd Bay

Caernarfon Castle

molluscs, while mussel beds occur in some of the flatter areas and these are sometimes dredged by trawlers, the metal mouths scraping the sea bed.

Edward I's imposing badge of oppression, the enormous and domineering castle at Caernarfon, pretty much dwarfs the river Seiont which flows to the sea in its shadow. It cost 12,000 pounds to build, using men and materials from all over – limestone from Anglesey, lime from Tenby, sea coal from Clwyd, lead from Snowdonia's mines, not to mention iron and steel from Newcastle-Under-Lyme, using sea craft and pack mules to transport the colossal quantities of building materials.

Edward wasn't just building a castle, he was building a reputation for himself, making himself the very stuff of legend. This would be achieved by plugging himself into ancient and very distinguished ancestry as he connected himself with the Emperor Maximus, who lived in Caernarfon and married Elen, the so-called Elen of the Hosts, who was the daughter of a British chief. For Edward to be able to underline his connection with this passage from the past, he claimed to have found the bones of a Roman emperor while they were excavating the foundations for his mighty castle, and mistakenly claimed it was none other than Constantine. Even if the connection was wrong, Edward set out to create his own Constantinople.

Like the capital of the Roman Empire in the east, his new castle had polygonal towers, not round ones and the patterned walls, with their bands of different coloured stone, are copies of the tile-laced walls of the Roman capital. This had a Golden Gate, so Edward had to have one too, and so Porth yr Aur, the gate of gold, was created. A stone eagle which features in the castle tower is the Imperial Eagle. This was a king trying so very hard to give himself the apparatus and authority of an emperor. He was taking Segontium, the Roman capital of North Wales and turning it into the seat of his own empire, connected of course to a

chain of other forbidding castles, designed to vanquish all hope of insurrection in the hearts of the troublesome Welsh.

Conveniently for a man who so loves the water, Alan Williams's office at Plas Menai, the National Watersports Centre, looks west onto the ever changing moods of the Menai, and the small church of Llanfairisgaer, which marks the spot where the Romans crossed over onto Anglesey, intent on taming the druids. This is how the historian Tacitus put it:

> Urged on by their general's appeals and mutual encouragements not to quail before a troop of frenzied women, they bore the standards onward, smote down all resistance, and wrapped the foe in the flames of his own brands. A force was next set over the conquered, and their groves, devoted to human superstitions, were destroyed. They deemed it, indeed, a religious duty to cover the altars with the blood of their captives and to consult the deities by inspecting human entrails.

There's much less bloodletting on Menai's shores nowadays and Alan loves this tidal waterway with its castles, views of mountains, wooded stretches, sandbanks and bridges. He thinks the

Alan Williams, sailor and sailing instructor

waters are alive: 'The Menai isn't to be taken lightly, she keeps you on your toes, has strong tides, and Atlantic storms can conspire to change her mood in an instant, when she can become a raging stretch of water, but fortunately, she can return to her tranquil self just as quickly. She can catch out the unprepared.'

Water has always played a part in Alan's life. He was born in a house on the beach in Crosby, Lancashire, his grandparents having emigrated from Hope and Rhoscolyn at the turn of the 20th century. In the early 1970s Crosby Council created a Marine Park, with a large lake at its heart. Alan built his first dinghy to sail there, enlisting the help of his woodworker dad, and soon the addiction to water craft developed and took hold. He graduated to racing them. Having been born with his feet back to front, Alan couldn't enjoy many traditional sports but one that involved sitting down suited him down to the ground, as it were.

On a sailing trip from Wales to Ireland in 1982 he had just left Port Dinorwig bound for Dublin when he noticed a new building being erected near Caernarfon. Little did he suspect that two years later he would be employed there as an instructor. Since when there has hardly been a day when he hasn't had some involvement with the Menai and it's little wonder that daughters Kate and Sarah have become sailing coaches, too. Not to forget Alan's wife, who is the team manager for the Great Britain junior sailing team, whose coach is Alan. Hopefully it makes married life a case of plain sailing.

Nowadays most people drive along the A55 at Penmaenmawr without giving a moment's thought to the great rocky mass above them. It's an invisible landscape. The village had over seventy shops in the 1930s and 1940s. It had quarrying and tourism, cheek by jowl. City dwellers from Liverpool were lured here by 'bracing and invigorating air, fresh pure mountain water, hills and the sea-shore.' There was work for those who wanted to stay longer. Yet above the terrace houses, pushed together like a concertina, there are evocative vistas of abandoned workings, rusted lengths of wire, drifts of scree and abandoned huts. Lush sprigs of heather counterpoint their blurts of purple against the igneous, granite grey. This is officially the source of the hardest rock in Britain, gouged and hewn from the mountain face, now pockmarked and brutalized by generations of labouring men. But slowly reverting back, with saplings claiming abandoned slopes, and crows on patrol.

Man has been working the rock here as far back as Neolithic times when there was nothing less than an axe factory in these high hills: the tools were taken wide and near, a historical hardware store, if you like. The modern quarry still exports stone far and wide, used in such schemes as the Mersey Tunnel

Anglesey from Caernarfon

and the Hamburg by-pass. After the Second World War no fewer than 1,100 men were employed at Penmaen and Graiglwyd quarries, days of stone crushing and cloying dust. But technology changed all that, as machines took the strain and slack and left men idle.

Conwy, like Caernarfon is dominated by its castle. In terms of fishing Conwy is noteworthy because it has historically been the centre of mussel gathering in Wales: there is even a Mussel Museum on the quay in the town. Literature underlines the longevity of the fishery here: there are some lines in Edmund Spenser's 'Faerie Queene' which refers to Conway,

> which out of his streame doth send Plenty of pearles
> to decke his dames withal

The river, which runs clear from its source, a small lake in the Migneint mountains north of Arennig Fawr, was still supplying pearls well into the 19th century when over four kilos of pearls were sent each week to London jewellers, with the sediment left after repeated washing of the mussels carefully separated with a feather to ensure that even the smallest pearl was harvested to adorn those 'dames'.

The number of mussel gatherers has declined nowadays with about twelve licenses granted each year to members of the four remaining families that still work the waters hereabouts. The season starts in late September when men go out in their own boats, taking with them rakes with long handles, originally designed by medieval monks, to help in the backbreaking work of picking up the molluscs, sometimes in the pitch darkness, or fog, or biting cold. Little wonder that mechanical dredging, and the farming of the river bed, with parts being harvested, are replacing raked mussels. The ones from deepest water are reputedly the best as they have been submerged in the water and so been

Chip van, Conwy

feeding all the time A local historian in *The History of the Town of Aberconwy*, published in 1835, gives details of the different types of mussels, some named after a flood, or *dilyw*, and others simply blue, or *glas*:

> There are two kinds of mussels found in the Conwy from which pearls are obtained: mya margaritifere (cragen y diluw) and the mytulis edulis (cragen lâs). Those of the former species are procured high up the river, about Trefriw, and pearls scarcely inferior to the oriental ones are occasionally found in them…
> The other variety, the cragen lâs, is found in abundance on the bar at the mouth of the river and great quantities of the mussels are gathered by numbers of industrious people.

Rumour has it that the largest pearl in the Crown of Britain comes from Conwy and was presented to Queen Elizabeth I by local landowner Sir John Wynne, though this is completely unsubstantiated. A good claim, though.

Above Penmaenmawr

Near Penamenmawr

Britannia Bridge

Yr Eifl and the Menai Strait

10 Conwy to Dee
The Richest Velvet Imaginable

Llandudno from the Great Orme

As prepossessing humps of rock go, it takes a lot to beat the Great Orme, or Pen-y-Gogarth. This limestone headland on the Creuddyn peninsula dominates the southern skyline of Llandudno, forcing one to crane one's neck at day's end to see the satsuma sun. Orme is a Viking name meaning serpent and this limestone mass is big enough to be as much kraken as snake. These rapacious Northern raiders might have given their name to the rock, but the town in its shadow takes its name from St Tudno, whose small church still stands in place on the head of the Orme, high enough to be closer to God but with commanding views over Snowdonia and the Conwy coast and even the distant prospect of the Strathclyde shore. On its cliffs guillemots and fulmars nest, summer visitors like the majority who come here.

In the Bronze Age the mines under the Orme were probably sufficiently busy to make Wales an important net exporter of copper.

It's a place surprisingly busy with buildings. There's the tramway, a lazy but elegant way to climb up past the community of copperworkers' cottages. What is today the summit complex building was originally 'The Telegraph Inn.' From here messages were relayed between Holyhead and Liverpool, advising of the imminent arrival of sailing ships laden with valuable cargo. During the Second World War it once more became a focus for signalling, this time as the RAF Great Orme Radar Station. Attempts to revive the golf club after the war failed, and the restored hotel was purchased by the middleweight boxer, Randolph Turpin. Turpin's bankruptcy led to suicide. It's a sad tale, of a man punched down by life and strife.

But the main reason for climbing the Orme is the view. Llandudno's hotels look like toys, but carefully arranged ones. The sea seems like a plane surface, as the waves are swallowed by the distance. A great black-backed gull flies past, its eyes at your level and when your gaze meets that of the bird there is the merest hint of recognition.

Stately Llandudno, self-styled Queen of the Resorts, with the regal facades of its hotels and succession of Bed and Breakfast signs, came into being in the mid 19th century, when local landowners, the Mostyn family, parcelled the land, opened it up for development and the first pier was built. It's a town with historical pedigree and colour – Australian premier Billy Hughes was born here, Charles Dodgson aka Lewis Carroll reputedly based his Alice on local girl Alice Liddell. Welsh nationalist firebrand Lewis Valentine preached at the town's

Llandudno

Llandudno

Tabernacl chapel. But it also has its modernity too, not least in the newly renovated Oriel Mostyn with its conceptual and contemporary art. Llandudno is a town of unhurried elegance and tea-cosy warmth with a huge appetite for full English breakfasts. In this properly groomed resort even the beach seems well combed, slicked down on either side by Brylcreemed slicks of seaweed.

If Llandudno is the Queen of Resorts then Rhyl is the knave, attracting not so much tourists as holiday makers, who double up as pleasure seekers, seeking it in the Monte Carlo Casino Lounge, the Honey Club and the XXX Licensed Adult Centre. It's all here, the route map to pleasure, and all painted with maritime gloss – from the Ocean City Chinese through to Geoff's Bait and Tackle.

On this December day, the promenade fun fair is quiet now, just a few wistful kids wishing it were August: the sea train under tarpaulin for the winter and the Aquablaster

hidden under flapping wraps. On the wall outside Cap'n Noahs, the over-optimistic slogan 'Sunny Rhyl' is somewhat dampened by what the Scots would call *haar* or sea-mist: odd how we in Wales, so often damply swaddled in such clammy weather, don't have our own word for it. The river Clwyd makes a rather ignominious entry into the sea, snaking past the artificial Marine Lake, with its hundred-year-old miniature railway. It's a narrow stretch of water separating Rhyl from its suburb of Kinmel Bay even though the gloss on both places is like cracked toenail enamel – Kiss Me Quick, Sun Centre, crisp battered fish and chips, bleeping arcade games, Fatty Arbuckles American Diner and the Seaquarium boasting 'the biggest lionfish in the world.'

In the summer months a tiny natural oasis away from the pulsing neon, arcade machine chatter and tattooed holiday-makers can be found at the Kinmel Dunes local nature reserve which, with its sand-hugging plants such as lucerne, rest-harrow, bird's foot trefoil and sea holly, protects fragments of what was once a monumental dune system. The holly, in particular, is worth pausing to look at as it's a beautiful plant. It's glaucous grey leaves speak of Arctic seas, and storm clouds made of lead.

Mostyn's port dates back four centuries to when the estuary was the key trading centre for the North West coastline. It was a haven for sailing ships navigating the estuary. Mostyn had several coalmines and, later, an ironworks.

Both industries flourished during the 19th century and by 1880 were providing work locally for 2,000 men. The site was one of the industrial powerhouses of north-east Wales. The ironworks closed as recently as 1961 and the works was dismantled four years later. Today, Mostyn is primarily an export port, shipping consignments of steel for Corus to customers around Europe, and handling other cargoes such as animal feed, fertiliser and aggregates.

The *Duke of Lancaster*

Sea access to Mostyn docks has for years been restricted by the need for ships to sail in at high tide, but now the port is able to offer ships the size of P&O's Irish Ferries round-the-clock access thanks to an intensive dredging programme, and its trading area extends as far as the eastern seaboard of the United States, West Africa and the Middle East. In 2004 the port experienced the loss of its ro-ro ferry service to Dublin but it luckily found other markets, in particular the shipment of Airbus A380 wings which are transported by barge from the Airbus factory at Broughton and transferred to ocean-going ships which then take them to Bordeaux.

In recent years, Mostyn has become a major player as a base for the Offshore Windfarm Construction and Support Industry. It has seen four major wind farms constructed from Mostyn over the last five years, the furthest away being Robin Rigg in the Solway Firth.

Just down the coast you encounter one of those optical illusions that never fails to delight, namely the sight of an enormous ship, the *Duke of Lancaster*, moored seemingly on dry land. Walk down the short length of path which runs alongside

the brook and you'll get up close to one of the final passenger-only railway steamers, built in 1956 and able to carry 600 first class and 1,200 second class passengers, as well as substantial cargoes. Now her cream hull is striated with rust and is wedged, by concrete, into her private dock. The ten lifeboats have died on their frozen stanchions, the flags long gone, even the heavy duty glass smithereened in places.

She started life as a cruise ship before becoming a ferry, though other vessels, designed to carry cars and passengers, were making ships such as the *Duke of Lancaster* redundant. She was finally retired in late 1978 though she was subsequently sold to a company called Empirewise of Liverpool who intended her to be used as a static ship at Llanerch-y-Môr, not far from the port of Mostyn in North Wales. The *Lancaster* arrived at her new home on the 10th of August, 1979, and has remained there ever since, beached off the River Dee and in an increasingly derelict state. Her intended use as a static leisure centre and market was relatively short-lived – she was known as 'The Fun Ship' and it was possible to visit the engine room and bridge. Plans for a 300-room hotel never appear to have got

Wind turbines and gas platform off Prestatyn

birds, the little tern, is now reduced to only one breeding colony in Wales, a sad contraction of range for a bird that formerly nested in many parts of the Welsh coast. The fact that the colony is on a popular beach right next door to busy caravan parks means that protecting them isn't easy. Keeping humans, and their four-legged friends, away is a job in itself, but then there are foxes to dissuade with the help of poultry netting and electric fences, and overly attentive crows to dissuade – although cutting down trees in the nearby caravan park has helped with this problem. On top of this there are the hazards of high tides and sandstorms during protracted gales to contend with.

Adrian has a real soft spot for little terns; he loves the jaunty, springy flight of these sea-swallows and also admires their pluckiness; often these small birds will chase birds of prey such as kestrels, even going as far as to angrily pluck out feathers. They also garner Adrian's respect because of the huge distances they cover – they fly from Gronant as far as north and west Africa.

In some years, such as 2010, the birds were very success-ful, with the colony producing 216 fledgelings, but ruefully he notes that in 2011 the birds really struggled, producing less than half that number. Kestrels must take the brunt of the blame, with at least 20 chicks being taken by what is, ironically, another protected species.

Adrian's enthusiasm for nature was fired as a six-year-old, when he started to discover the wildlife around his home in Dolgellau. Spotting peregrine falcons was a real delight, although he's revised his opinion of them a little since then having had to physically chase them away when they were attacking terns at the colony on the rim of Cemlyn lagoon on Anglesey when he was a warden there.

But now summer is long gone and the year is dying. I find myself on the edge of the Dee on the last day of December,

further than the preliminary planning stage however, and it was not long before the ship closed for business.

The coastal stretch from Point of Ayr down towards Flint offers plentiful vantage points for seeing birdlife, and the Dee estuary can be teeming with it.

Adrian Hibbert sometimes hears terns calling when there are no terns, a sure sign that he's spent a little too much time in their company. As a Countryside Warden for Denbighshire County Council one of his duties is protecting the tern colony at the shingle beach of Gronant, east of Rhyl. One of our rarest sea-

Little tern

one of those days with little daylight that pass on silent wings like soot-coloured owls. It is a day for pondering the variety of greys – battleship, pewter and fog – that meld together in winter's landscape.

My good friend Iolo Williams and I once spent just such a day searching for snow buntings near Abergele, another crabby day in bleak midwinter, all diminished light and insistent drizzle. We hithered and thithered here and there to no avail. Then, having given up the ghost and taken our sandwiches back to the car, there they were! Snow buntings, a dozen or more, pecking for seeds on a shingle bank in the light of the headlamps. A whole, beautiful flake of them, a flurry of them, both snowy and showy. Serendipity has a big part to play in watching birds, or, as a great poet once said 'A rare bird is only rare when you're not there.' We pulled out gently, not keen to run one over.

It's low tide at the RSPB's Point of Ayr reserve. Gronant dunes and Talacre Warren form the last remnant of a dune system that once extended along the length of the North Wales coast. It's important for species other than terns, such as sand lizards, sandhill rustic moths and natterjack toads: indeed four new ponds have been excavated in November to help this latter species. What looks like an infantry battalion plods across the sands, en route for a warming cup of char in one of the Talacre caffs. There's been a fishing competition and each man seems to be carrying an enormous amount of equipment, as if they were planning to be out at water's edge for a week. When I ask the obvious question they all seem pleased, for today there were plenty of whitings and dabs out there. I congratulate them one and all. One crunches across new deposits of razor shells to the spit of land that forms one of the most important high tide roosts for waders on the Dee.

When the tide is up, this is an avian air show, all whirling, twisting and flashing wings as wading birds bank and veer, before they turn and settle nervously. One of the specialties of the Dee is the knot, a slightly dumpy grey bird that is incredibly sociable: you hardly ever see one by itself, as this is a species that must stick together. They can seem to carpet the mud, as they prog and probe for one of their favourite food items, namely the Baltic tellin, a pink-shelled bivalve found here in enormous numbers, hence the concentrations of knots. But there are plenty of other species too, all jockeying for position and a safe place to stand, often on one leg, away from the rising waters.

Adrian Hibbert, Countryside Warden

Having read one of the warning signs on the way here, I stick to the edge of the dunes: it told you what to do in case of stepping into quick sand: 'Step slowly back the way you came... If you sink further, lie back and slowly release your legs and use a back stroke motion until you reach firmer ground.' Memories of being in just such a predicament flood back, the very idea sucking at my wellingtons. The sand was a pair of gigantic lips, eager to digest me, suck me down so that not even the occipital lobe of my skull showed where I had once been.

The Dee estuary is a glistening brown expanse of faraway river and wet mud seemingly covered with a gargantuan polythene sheet. There are small gatherings of shelduck parading as they feed, showy and highly visible. Maybe the fact they don't taste all that good makes them confident.

And so to the last port of call. This coastal walk started at one mighty estuary, the Severn and concludes at another, the Dee, and I have parked the car between Flint Castle and the lifeboat station, overlooking Flint Sands across toward Neston and Parkgate on the English side of the estuary. Hilbre island is slowly being lapped by waves and being cut off.

I splosh across the wet grassland in front of the castle and a pair of snipe skyrocket away, so well camouflaged I don't see so much as a feather's worth of warning. This section of walk has been generally improved as part of the Welsh Assembly Government's all-Wales coastal path, so there are ample opportunities to pause awhile and learn about the history of this stretch. Flint Dock, now a muddy culvert, albeit with a channel of deep water slicing through, was built in the 1800s to export Halkyn Mountain Lead and soon afterwards a colliery on the marsh started to produce coal.

The existence of the quay attracted the attention of a rather dastardly sounding chemist called James Muspratt, who established a chemical works here, having been hounded out of Liverpool for 'pollution and public nuisance.' At its peak 2,000 people were employed here making soda: the air hereabouts was a toxic swirl, dusty and yellow with fumes, including hydrochloric acid. From the 1900s onwards the area was given over to the enormous Courtaulds factory, which in its heyday employed 4,000 workers and was Flint's main employer until the factory gates were shut forever in 1977.

It's quieter now, given over to dog walking and families pushing baby buggies. There are plenty of parents getting over the Christmas stuffing.

I sit on Flint Point, looking out over Flint Marsh. It's high tide: 7.9 metres at twenty past two in the afternoon.

Now the estuary is millpond still, a Zen quality to the elegant rafts of duck drifting along mid-river eddies. Black headed gulls give one squawking, raucous cheer as they discover some last morsels of afternoon tea before they too drift down onto the glassy surface, now turning into bottle-green stains and slicks. A small flock of teal play aerial Twister overhead before they settle in a thin creek that dissects the marsh in front of me.

This part of the coast is built up and built upon from Flint to the English border, with Connah's Quay gas power station, the steelworks at Shotton and the rather graceful Flintshire Bridge which is the largest asymmetric cable stay bridge in Britain, its span hemmed in by plentiful electricity pylons because of not one but two power stations nearby.

The English side of the Dee is a thickening charcoal line and some small white boats seem as if they'll be the last things to disappear as the light diminishes, as if their hulls are able to attract the last photons of the day. It is all turning into a Whistler Nocturne as the estuary settles into silence. Grey darkens. A single redshank sounds shrilly as if to emphasize the way the quiet replaces its echo. Night extends its cloak over the marshlands. It looks like the richest velvet imaginable.

Conwy estuary

Stone graffiti, the Great Orme

Rhyl

Oystercatchers, Point of Ayr

Dee Bridge

Wales at Water's Edge

A Photographer's Afterword

The intention of this book was to illuminate both Wales and 'Welshness' through the mirror, or prism, of its shoreline. It examines all aspects of the coastline, so conventionally unpromising man-made subject matter has been sought as well as the stunning landscapes that Wales is rightly renowned for. It would be impossible to do justice to the subject without tackling both. As a consequence the book has become both a document of its subject matter and also an exploration of our relationship with nature.

The two years I worked on these photographs were truly a voyage of discovery. The Welsh coast is something like 1700 miles long if you include the islands, so it could hardly have been otherwise. But just as exciting sometimes was the realisation that I had photographed a familiar location in an unfamiliar way.

During work on the book I became aware of the term 'psychogeography' and as a psychology graduate with an interest in all things geographical, I was intrigued. The word seems to have as many definitions as users, which have included architects, anarchists, philosophers and particularly writers. But never photographers.

A distillation of the many possible meanings of the term psychogeographer might be 'urban wanderer as author',

and writers such as Will Self and Iain Sinclair have been described as such. The elasticity of the definition has also allowed the inclusion of the rural writer Alfred Watkins into the genre and also the film-maker Patrick Keiller, director of the 'Robinson' trilogy. His subject matter is gently and perceptively political and both urban and rural..

One definition of psychogeography suggests it is a study of 'the confluence of people and place, the manner in which our environment impacts upon us and vice versa.' Who better to tackle this than the photographer? Yet to my knowledge the term has never been so used.

In a review of one of my earlier books, it was noted that the photographs in it could have been taken by several different photographers. I suspect this was not meant as a compliment! But different subjects demand different approaches. In this book some of the images have been obtained in a highly structured fashion. Given that I live about 100 miles away, it would have been impossible to photograph the fishermen of the Severn estuary or the falcon at Lamby Way landfill, for example, without making arrangements with certain people at certain dates and times.

But many of the photographs were the result of plonking myself in a location then just walking and looking. Quite often the makings of a photograph seemed to reach my consciousness from peripheral vision (or elsewhere) as my mind wandered. This would, I feel, be the work of a psychogeographer in the purest form of the word – a direct response to one's surroundings.

Having found a location it would sometimes be necessary to return at a different time of day – or year – to catch it when the light was at its best. This would be the classical modus operandi of the landscape photographer. But in reality very few of the images here would fit completely into any one of these three approaches and most have aspects of two or all within them.

To be honest I have become tired of using the term 'landscape photographer' to describe myself, because it has become rather a straightjacket. These days only certain types of landscape seem admissible – wild places (or at least superficially wild), and 'golden hour' light. Certain types of equipment, such as ten stop neutral density filters, ultra wide-angle lenses, and sometimes high levels of digital manipulation seem de rigueur. These things may have their place, of course, and the results are often stunningly beautiful, but they are the landscape seen through rose-tinted spectacles.

During the project I began working with new subject matter altogether, such as portraiture and wildlife. It gave me the confidence I needed to photograph people. And while I have been interested in wildlife for as long as I've been interested in photography, I've not seriously attempted to combine the two until very recently.

On many occasions my experience of being on the coast was enlivened by the arrival of that 'commendable crow', the chough. These special birds seem to bring a special place alive with their presence, and, indeed, some not quite so special places – they have a particular liking for abandoned buildings and quarries. The chough became a symbol of the Welsh coastline for me.

Jeremy Moore

Acknowledgements

My thanks go particularly to Jon Gower, whose delightful text complements the images so well. I'm grateful that at Gomer, Mairwen Prys Jones and her successor Dylan Williams had faith in the project, whilst Ceri Wyn Jones helped to pull all the disparate strands together. Others to whom I'm indebted are Rebecca Ingleby Davies of mopublications, and those whose portraits are reproduced in this book, including the Lave Net fishermen and Martin Morgan. Also helpful were Jonathan Hutchings and George Harvey of Cardiff City Council, John Owens of Falconry Services; the Glandyfi purse-seine net fisherman Geraint Lewis and son Jake; Matt Richards of BAM Nuttall; Alastair Moralee of the RSPB; Shelagh Hourahane; Nigel Nicholas, and Jane MacNamee. Photographic books about the Welsh coast by Andy Davies, Peter Watson and Aled Rhys Hughes were also valuable reference points. Finally many thanks to Roger Thomas and all at CCW, whose enthusiasm and funding allowed the project to go ahead.

JM

This book is the product of walking and reading, drawing on books such as Ian Skidmore's *Gwynedd*, Aled Ellis and Nan Griffiths's *Minffordd: Rhwng Dau Draeth* and Jonah Jones's book about Clough Williams-Ellis. I was also lucky enough to present a TV series about Pembrokeshire while writing this present volume, so thanks to Lona Llewelyn Davies for that opportunity. Thanks also to all the people I met along the way, who shared their love of place and space, not least Jeremy Moore himself. And most of all to Sarah, Elena and Onwy, who came with me to Aberdaron, where we saw how the land ends.

JG

Bardsey Island

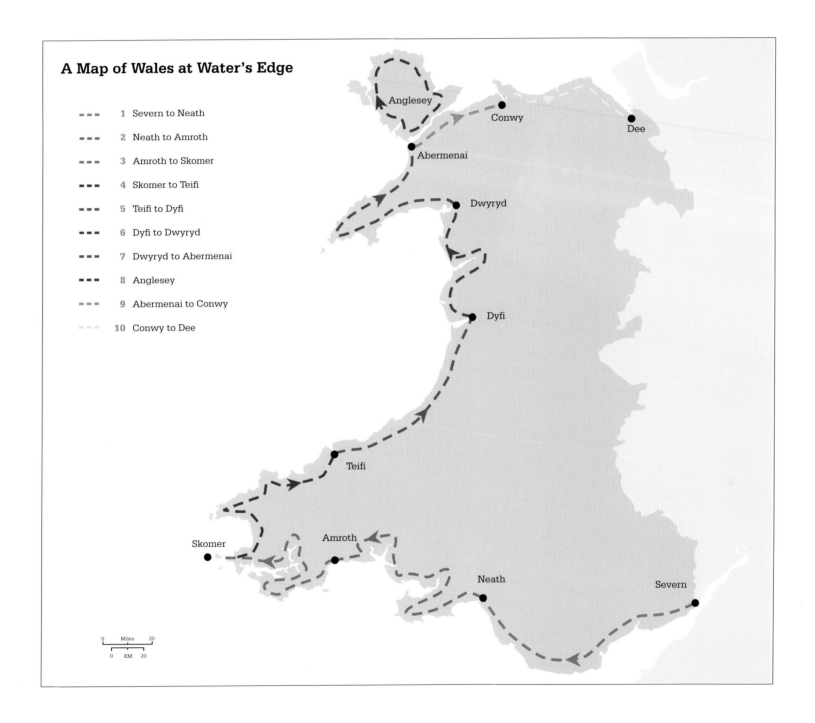

A Map of Wales at Water's Edge

Anglesey

Conwy

Dee

Abermenai

Dwyryd

Dyfi

Teifi

Skomer

Amroth

Neath

Severn

0   Miles   20

0   KM   20